CW00504853

BECOMING A
3D CEO

The ultimate guide to
unleashing your inner leader

Luis Alvarez Satorre

Becoming a 3D CEO

First published in 2018 by

Panoma Press Ltd
48 St Vincent Drive, St Albans, Herts, AL1 5SJ, UK
info@panomapress.com
www.panomapress.com

Book layout by Neil Coe.

Printed on acid-free paper from managed forests.

ISBN 978-1-784521-39-4

Printed and bound in Great Britain by TJ International Ltd.

ACKNOWLEDGEMENTS

Writing a book is a fascinating adventure. I was impressed to have so many people involved, helping and challenging me to make it better.

I should start by saying thank you to my wife, Queca, who encouraged me to share all the lessons learned and stories of these years of experience. Her support, ideas and inspirational challenge throughout the process, as a beta reader and a listener to my reflections, have made this book a better one.

Thank you to my kids and their partners who have listened patiently to my considerations about the book at its different stages.

Thank you to my father who, when the book was almost ready, asked me for the three reasons for writing the book. He made me think. My answer? "Understanding what it takes to be a CEO, inspiring people to reflect on their current situation, and encouraging them to act on that new small idea they could find in the book."

Thank you to Tim Webber, Eduardo Ruiz, father and son, and Carmen Quiñones who read my first manuscript. Their honest feedback made me reconsider the structure and focus the content.

Thank you to Mindy Gibbins-Klein and the Panoma Press team who drove a flawless process to make this happen. Their coaching conversations and solid methodology facilitated the outcome that is in your hands now.

Thank you to Sinead Faherty who carefully translated some of my 'Spanglish' expressions into a more readable English version.

Thank you to my beta readers who generously dedicated time to go through the pages, providing valuable feedback. To Victor Bravo, a friend, a colleague and a companion in many of the stories you find here. His encouragement but also his criticisms contributed definitively to enrich the final text. To Rodolfo Carpentier, Joy McCormack, Claire Mason, Maria Grazia Pecorari, Conor O'Neill and Miguel Alvarez who backed the skills, principles and lessons presented here, as well as questioning, challenging and pushing me to make them more compelling, clear and exciting.

To Gary Heffernan, who kindly endorsed this book with his valuable perspectives.

Thank you to all my friends and colleagues who are the real authors of this book. Everything here has been possible because of the experiences we lived together. We experienced incredible growth journeys and we faced some difficult moments. We all learned from each of those. But one thing lasts: our relationships.

CONTENTS

INTRODUCTION

The lessons you learn are the most important assets you accumulate to shape you as a person. I have collected a good number and I wanted to share them. Why? First, because I would have loved to find a book like this when I started. Second, if anything I have learned could help anyone to make better decisions, or become a better leader, my effort would have been worth it. Third, it has been a marvellous excuse to reflect on and align many ideas, actions and stories, and it has been a unique opportunity to keep learning as part of this reflective process. You never stop learning. Finally, it has been a way of saying thank you to those who have accompanied me on this fascinating journey. They will recognise themselves in some of the experiences, stories or projects that we encountered together. My family, my friends and my colleagues are all the indirect authors of this book.

Let me start by going back to my childhood. My memories of my father's work are dominated by his enthusiasm for what he was doing: from opening a new exchange to provide telephone connections to a new village to, later in his career, creating a marketing and services platform to convert traditional telephone subscribers into real customers. I learned that passion for what you do is an essential component of living an enjoyable life. When I was a teenager, any conversation I had with him about future studies, jobs or interests almost always ended with his statement: "Whatever you do, aim to do it at your best." Some people say that the passion I put into my work is to make sure I stick to that advice.

In my days as a CEO, I realised that I have also kept the same inspiration from my mother, to live life with intensity. Her heart disease, which ended her life when she was only 63, was not an obstacle to getting up in the morning and doing things whenever she had some fresh energy.

The root of what we do and how we act was really created a long time ago, in our childhoods. Consciously or unconsciously, it affects how we live our lives, how we face challenges, and how we deal with our daily tasks. However, there are many aspects that can be identified, learned, adjusted, improved or even changed. You find role models, or people who inspire you. Whether that's a well-known figure such as Mandela, or someone close to you – in my case, my wife is a constant source of inspiration and support.

I am a proud engineer, passionate about technology and how it changes the way we live and work. I believe in people and in the power of teams to transform organisations. I love working with customers, discovering how your business can become an extension of theirs. I enjoy the challenges that new generations put in front of us and the opportunities created by the disruption that new operating models bring, and I am convinced of our unlimited capacity to learn and develop.

I realised, in my 30 years' of experience leading teams, that leadership is one aspect we all want to learn and develop, and one of the best roles to display that leadership is the role of the Chief Executive Officer. I experienced that when in my career I became CEO, first of a country operation and later of a multibillion business within BT, a global telecommunications leader, providing services to companies and governments around the globe.

However, I found that, in truth, it is a multifaceted job. It challenges your personal and professional skills to the limit, and it forces you to get better every day if you are determined to succeed. Those different facets of the role are what I have called the three dimensions of the CEO, and this is what this book is about: evangelism, engagement and execution.

In the first chapter, I encourage you to reflect on why you might want to be a CEO. Next, I present the core skills I believe are required to be a successful 3D CEO, and then I discuss how they can be applied to the most critical areas of the job. While each chapter has a stronger association with one of the three dimensions, several core skills should be used to perform at your best.

I discuss how to deploy those skills to:

- create the vision for your company

- engage with all kind of stakeholders

- leverage the power of your team

- build a customer-obsessed organisation

- drive a high-performance culture

- stay focused

- be the change

I will share lessons I learned in great and in difficult moments. I will share some recommendations, strategies and tips about what it takes to be a CEO. The stories you will find in the book try to illustrate and bring to life those ideas and concepts. But I will also try to give you, the reader, the opportunity to reflect on how you would face similar challenges yourself. Or how the organisation you work in would act under those circumstances.

It doesn't matter whether you are already a CEO, you have the ambition to be, you manage a team, or you are just curious about what it takes. This book is for you. It is my intention that you enjoy reading it as much as I enjoyed writing it for you.

A couple of notes before you begin:

As I am a man, I have written 'he' when referring to my experiences as a CEO. But please read 'he' or 'she'.

At the end of each chapter, I have added reflections or questions to provoke thought. They are opportunities to think about your own way of developing, and so you might prefer to break and reflect on some of those queries.

First reflection

Think about, and try to write down, what are your roots, your references, why you act the way you do.

To go a step further, write what you would like to learn from this book.

CHAPTER I

DISCOVER THE
THREE-DIMENSIONAL CEO

I learned that leadership is something we all need – and use – in all areas of life. Whether you are playing football, building a family or planning a trip and whether you are heading up a project, leading a team or becoming a manager. I have found that you need a set of distinct leadership skills, all associated with three main dimensions, which interrelate, reinforce and develop together. The better you are at each of them, the better you are at leading. Personally, I found these three dimensions essential as a CEO and this is what I call the 'three-dimensional CEO'.

Understand the three-dimensional CEO

The journey to becoming a CEO is full of lessons that are key to remember and absorb. I found that they prepare you for the job, but never enough. Once you have started, the learning curve only accelerates. In my experience, there are three hidden CEO roles underneath the well-known banner of the Chief Executive Officer – three dimensions of leadership. Each is essential in certain moments. How much weight you put on each of them will drive your success.

The three roles are: Chief Evangelist Officer, Chief Engagement Officer, and Chief Execution Officer.

The Chief Evangelist Officer is responsible for creating a vision for the organisation: generating excitement, making it memorable, and linking the intellectual and the emotional side of the team. He must define what he wants his long-term legacy to be. He should consolidate the values of the organisation. He must connect the market and customers with his vision, but at the same time, listen to the market and refine that vision, adjusting to a constantly changing digital world. Traditionally, the vision was created at the top and cascaded down. Nowadays, co-creation is the key. It means involving your employees, your customers and your stakeholders in building the vision.

The Chief Engagement Officer is the one who must connect the dots between the vision and the execution. The vision is nothing without a team who believe in it and the execution is nothing without the team who deliver it. Leading by example, the CEO should drive customer obsession within the organisation. He should do everything in his power to recruit and develop the right team, empowering them, and aligning the right incentives and recognition. He should make his team feel proud to deliver, so that he is not simply using the organisation as a means to achieve the vision, he is bringing together a group of people to achieve a common goal.

The Chief Execution Officer must translate the vision into actual plans. He must define the outcomes, the metrics, the key performance indicators, work the details, ensure that tools are available, put in place the right governance and track the performance against those goals. He is the one who should drive change across the organisation, staying focused to guarantee the full delivery of the vision.

The integrated work of these three roles is what will make the CEO and, more importantly, the organisation, a success. Also, it is important to link these three dimensions to who you are as a person, understanding why you do what you do.

Recently, I had the opportunity to attend a lunch with a few people in New York, including Dr Henry Kissinger, an American diplomat and political scientist best known as a former US Secretary of State. It was a privilege to share a table with him. At one point, we were discussing around our table what Artificial Intelligence (AI) is bringing to our businesses and society. AI has a positive side, supporting our learning in many areas such as health or business. But it also has its risks, affecting certain jobs or creating unintended consequences. In one of his interventions, Dr Kissinger asked: "Maybe we should reflect on why we are doing this? Why are we developing AI?"

There are many answers to this question, from improving efficiency to simply challenging our ability to innovate. But it made me think. It is true that, sometimes, we develop technologies or solutions without a clear vision of what we are trying to achieve. The speed at which we operate could make us lose sight of our actual purpose. So, it is always worth asking yourself why you do what you do.

In summary, the Chief Evangelist Officer's job is closely tied to what the CEO believes in, what motivates him, what makes him proud, and what makes him happy. I enjoyed the experience of continuously learning about myself.

The Chief Engagement Officer's job brings together the CEO's soft skills, the intangible assets, building empathy as a key element of his relationships. It is well reflected in this famous sentence from Benjamin Franklin: "Tell me and I forget, teach me and I remember, involve me and I learn." Involvement is the first step towards driving engagement. People and the connections I built made me feel energised and ready to face any challenge.

The Chief Execution Officer relies on the CEO's hard skills, those focused on tangible outcomes. His success depends on his responsiveness to the challenges and opportunities he faces, which tools, techniques and methods he masters to make things happen. I felt proud when looking at the results we produced as a team.

The circumstances, and how you act under them, will determine how much you decide to show of each of the three. Let me illustrate how a newly appointed CEO decided to involve his organisation to create and develop its vision.

When Joe Garner was appointed CEO of Nationwide, his job was not about making a big turnaround. He had to simply continue the solid performance and trajectory the building society had been displaying. However, in the changing environment of the financial services industry, Joe needed everybody engaged in the challenges they were facing. Joe is an active blogger and a firm believer in the people's voice. So, he launched 'The Big Conversation', a series of face-to-face feedback sessions and surveys to refine the purpose, the mission and vision for Nationwide over the coming years.

The team collected over 20,000 pieces of feedback and consolidating those views helped to produce a solid set of outcomes. Joe and his team brought together over 13,000 employees to share the results of the joint work, clearly outlining both the challenges and the aspirations for the future. 'The Big Conversation' drove a better understanding of the collective ambition so that there was, consequently, a stronger focus on execution.

Know why you want to be a CEO

The journey to becoming a CEO has some key moments and turning points. One of them is the personal decision of wanting to be a CEO. You must reflect whether or not you really want it, and why; if you really, truly want to be, it is possible. But there are a lot of trade-offs to make, particularly around how you like to spend your time, and how you focus your efforts. Deciding to be a CEO is not good or bad; it has to do more with what you actually want out of life. In my personal experience, it is an exciting and rewarding job but it is also a tough and challenging one.

When thinking about the reasons why you would like to opt for such a position, you need an immense degree of honesty and self-assessment. Let me share three risks and three opportunities I considered when faced with being a CEO.

The greatest risks are when someone would love to be CEO because of how it would look to the rest of the world. There is no doubt that the role is associated with power, social recognition in the business community, and making money.

Firstly, having power means 'being the boss'. Having the ability to decide and execute what you think is right. Having authority. Power is connected to the job you hold. As long as you are in post, you have the power. But the risk is that you could make decisions considering you are right, just because you are the CEO. You risk becoming surrounded by people who don't like to contradict you because you hold the baton. The 'possession of the truth' could separate you gradually from the real world and impact the quality of your decisions.

Secondly, social recognition in the community can be attractive, and being appreciated by your business colleagues or the society is not bad at all. But having people around praising you because of the job you have is a risk. It is tempting to think that you are your job and this can become your main reason to be, or remain, a CEO. The risk is that in order to keep this sense of recognition, you make decisions that are not necessarily the right ones from a long-term perspective. It is important to remember who you are, to keep yourself separate from the job, so that you do not trade business focus for your own external presence. Otherwise your ego will get in the way of running the organisation as you should.

Finally, money is an obvious motivation for taking a CEO job. CEO rewards are higher as, in most cases, it is a highly exposed job that should bring a significant contribution by creating value for the business and the society. But good corporate governance helps to make sure reward is fairly aligned to a CEO's actual achievement; money is not associated with the job title alone. In any case, if making money is your main motivation, I must say that it is not worth it.

On the other hand, the greatest opportunities of being a CEO are mainly to do with what you achieve for others. You have the opportunity to have an impact in the society, the industry or the company, and to drive value creation for all stakeholders. But you can also reach a personal pride and sense of achievement.

Firstly, you can make a big impact, whether you are developing a new product strategy, making a difference for your customers, transforming the core business, or developing industry leadership; creating new jobs, expanding operations to other markets, or influencing the community in which the organisation operates. The CEO should consider the kind of impact he wants to make. This must be included as part of the vision, as a constant guide for the CEO's actions.

Secondly, when I refer to value creation, this is a more tangible way of measuring the impact. It has to do with the incremental value that the CEO is able to generate as a consequence of implementing a clear and solid vision and strategy. The share price is the obvious measure if it is a public company, or simpler metrics such as additional enterprise value. However, it can also be associated to growth in specific metrics – including certain portfolio areas, the number of customers, the number of contracts signed – which can provide sustainability to the business. In some difficult cases, it can be related to a major restructuring to help a business survive and recover. In summary, value creation reflects the contribution of the CEO and his team while driving the organisation towards the vision.

Finally, there is no greater personal reward than the sense of achievement. Reaching the job of CEO is difficult, and staying in the job is even more challenging. The appointment is a consequence of what you have done so far and, more importantly, the confidence others have in what you will deliver. This significant demonstration of trust should make you feel proud. And defining your ambitions for the organisation, and identifying those targets clearly, will only add to it. This sentiment is something that will stay with you for a long time after you have left the CEO role. This is what I call the 'sense of achievement'.

So, when you consider being a CEO, or taking any senior position, make sure you have thought it through fully. The more you minimise the risks and strengthen the opportunities I mentioned, the more satisfied you will be and the larger the impact you will make.

One summer, I got a call from the CEO of the company I was working for. He offered me an executive committee position leading one of the divisions of the group. It was a more technical, internally focused division, one that I was not as close to. I draw my energy from working with customers, so while it was a brilliant opportunity to progress to a higher level in the organisation, it was not my preferred option.

I declined the offer. It was a difficult decision. But I explained it well to the CEO: I felt I could make a higher impact with the global, customer-facing position I had at the time.

Eighteen months later, I was offered the top leadership of the global, customer-facing division. Stick to what you believe and what aligns with your motives and sources of energy.

Reflection

We have discussed the three dimensions of leadership and how each contributes to the overall CEO role.

Reflecting on those three dimensions:

- Which one are you best at?
- Which one do you enjoy the most?
- Which one would people around you recognise as your most remarkable one? Why?
- Which dimension are you determined to develop?

Considering the reasons to be a CEO:

- Do you recognise those risks and opportunities in the way you look at jobs?
- Do you think your CEO has the right balance?
- Or, if you are the CEO, do you think you have the right balance?

CHAPTER II

DEVELOP THE CORE SKILLS
OF THE 3D CEO

During these years as a CEO, I have learned that there are a few core skills that have helped me to do a better job. This list gives you those core skills that I believe are key to succeed and they underpin the three dimensions of the role. Everything starts with you. Your knowledge, understanding and self-awareness will be the foundation of what you will achieve. You should build on your strengths, minimise the impact of your weaknesses and develop new capabilities. You are on a mission for which you need to be well equipped. These are some essential core skills to master, and you will need to learn how and when to use them. It is a fascinating journey of learning, personal growth and opportunities to make an impact in your company and your society. Your determination to succeed will make it possible.

The 3D CEO – Core Skills

EXECUTION SKILLS

Resilient

Focused

ENGAGEMENT SKILLS

Connected

Inspiring

EVANGELIST SKILLS

Strategic thinker

Empathetic

Balanced   Obsessed

Curious listener

Passionate   Positive

Entrepreneur

Bold

Humble to learn

Unreasonable

II.I. EVANGELIST DIMENSION. YOUR INNER SKILLS

The Evangelist dimension is at the centre of how you behave and perform. These skills are the ones that you will develop for yourself. To some extent, they will be developed when you are alone and they prepare you for the external interactions you will have. You should be a strategic thinker, passionate about what you do, obsessed with doing the right things, positive about how you look around you, and personally balanced.

II.I.a STRATEGIC THINKER

I consider strategic thinking an essential capability. It is fundamental to develop the vision. By thinking strategically, you will look into the future. You should design it, rather than waiting for it to happen. Thinking means reflection. It is spending quality time considering options, evaluating alternatives and getting inputs from several sources. You should be able to construct the model of the company in your brain. The highest levels of this power will be reached when you can explain complexity in simple words, when you can describe your business in an easy way. One of my bosses, early in my career, told me: "I like the way you provide simple explanations of complicated problems. Make sure you keep this ability and develop it. It will help you and, more importantly, many others." So I did.

Having the architecture of the organisation and how your business operates in your mind will allow you to define its future shape. You can create the vision. A vision based on facts which, by taking a realistic and ambitious approach, describes the desired outcome. It should also be co-created with your team, involving all possible stakeholders.

Strategic thinking requires you to correlate facts and circumstances around you. There will be events in the market, moves by your competitors, projects in other areas of your business, which will show new and unpredicted scenarios. New opportunities will emerge and risks will be more visible to you. This privileged perspective from the top will permit you to modify the course of your corporate journey.

To master it, you should incorporate new technologies into your thinking process. We live in a digital world and it will become even more so in future. Becoming a digital leader will help you to have a more robust strategic thinking process.

In my job as CEO, at a time when we were discussing how to drive growth for the coming years, I felt I needed time to think. We had a good set of data and a lot of presentations about opportunities and new areas to explore. But I needed time to think, and in complicated busy diaries it is always difficult to find a slot. So, for two weeks I booked an hour every morning with myself. For the first hour of every day I went through the information, read some external reports and pondered the different alternatives.

We had three possible ways to expand our business. First, increase share of wallet from our existing customers. Second, enlarge our portfolio of services. Third, extend our operations to other geographies. But we could not afford to execute the three of them simultaneously. Taking time to think really helped me to follow up the discussion with the team and make the final decision. We focused on existing customers with a controlled set of additional investments in new products, and we postponed any geographical expansion.

II.I.b OBSESSED

Most business leaders I know have an obsession. It can be explicit in how they behave, or it could just be how they feel inside. However, a successful CEO should be obsessed – in a constructive way, of course. And it is possible: obsession with providing the highest level of service, obsession with winning in the market, obsession with recruiting the best talent. You should develop a fanatic belief in your core principles, live your values and execute considering every single detail. I was obsessed with continuously improving our business, always aiming to do better.

One year, to have a refreshed perspective of the business, we took the top 100 jobs of the organisation and we declared them open for applications. Then, we asked all the managers holding these roles to apply for any two of the positions. We ended with circa one third of them in new roles. This rotation generated a renewed energy in the team. Our obsession with improving made this initiative possible.

Being obsessed means being ready to do a forensic analysis of problems or opportunities when it is needed. It represents the constant watch of competitors. It consists of those small details that make a big difference when it comes to serving customers.

The CEO of a large global bank told me he was obsessed with providing good service to customers. During a visit to one of his branches, the branch manager said that there were some complaints from customers on how their account statements were printed. The CEO asked to be shown some examples. They were taken to the IT department and when inspecting the issue, they found a simple problem: they were using low-cost ink cartridges that were printing some dirty statements when they contained a lot of text. Not only that, the issue was happening in other branches. So, they changed the ink cartridge supply in all branches, and the quality of printed documents improved everywhere. Every detail counted for him when it came to driving his obsession for customer service.

II.I.c POSITIVE

I have always aimed to develop a positive mindset, to generate positivity around me. Being positive is not about being deluded, losing touch with reality if it gets tough. It means taking a proactive attitude about the art of the possible. It is about being ready to enjoy the good things that are happening. Saying thank you; being grateful to people, customers or suppliers; recognising the contribution of individuals or teams. Being positive is about smiling and looking at the bright side of life. It is about believing in people, supporting them and expecting good reactions.

Challenges become opportunities under a positive mindset. Applying this mentality can make the impossible possible. Having discussions, addressing problems and looking at new ideas with a confident perspective will facilitate better outcomes. It will generate a can-do attitude when dealing with issues. Challenges will be barriers to overcome rather than insurmountable obstacles.

In one of our senior management team events we presented what we called 'The Impossible Club'. It was designed to inspire the team to lead with a positive mindset and inspiring others to never give up. As a symbol of this mindset, each of them had to write their name on a piece of paper and put it into a ballot box if they were ready to become 'members of the club'. We continued to use this can-do attitude in many conversations when we were discussing difficult problems.

But keeping a positive spirit is not easy. I found that it must be a heavily internalised power. There will always be strong headwinds to manage in your role, which will put your confidence at risk. Your ability to remain consistent, and to remain confident about the future and your ability to manage the headwinds, will be key.

It is important to give realistic messages about business performance. I balanced the positive approach with transparency and clarity of the facts. It would be a big mistake to share results with a positive perspective if they are not good enough. However, you can always highlight areas of progress. These will always help to create confidence in the future. Ultimately, your positivity should not obscure difficult situations but it should help to get through them. Credibility is key.

I remember a time when there was a significant issue in some of the data centre services in one of our older locations. Some customers were not getting the quality they were expecting, and we were not happy either. I had a meeting with one of them and it was a tough conversation; their external website had been affected, and so had their end customers. We took a proactive attitude: we recognised the issue and we apologised, but we also presented a plan to recover and transform the situation. We asked for their involvement and clearly demonstrated our confidence in our ability to deliver. A few months after the incident, I met the same customer once again. They were pleased about the service, but even more importantly, they called out our positive attitude, even when facing such an issue.

A positive can-do approach will make a difference to everyone around you.

II.I.d PASSIONATE

Passion has been a distinctive skill in my career. To deal with challenges, enjoy opportunities, drive transformation and lead your team, you need to have passion for your job. The CEO role demands high energy levels, all the time. The stamina needed for such a demanding position must come from your innermost beliefs. Passion is about putting your heart behind your actions and commitments.

Everyone, employees and customers alike, will feel your passion for the business. It will be noticed as a core element to deliver the company purpose, the contribution to society and the desire to make an impact. Your eyes, your tone of voice and your body language will transmit it.

It demonstrates that you are fully embedded in the task of being a successful CEO. You cannot make trade-offs when taking the role. You should love it, otherwise you will struggle. You might survive but you won't enjoy it. Being fully into it, without restrictions, is mandatory if you want to have the best experience as a CEO and generate the largest impact.

I felt that passion for my CEO role. I used to say that I would do 80% of the job for free. The joy of meeting customers, working hand in hand with your team, innovating by creating new services – these are unique opportunities.

When I was appointed, I had a long conversation with my boss about my plans and ideas about the main priorities to address. We were going through some of the details of my first 90 days plan that I had prepared. At the end of our chat, he asked me how I was feeling. I said: "I feel privileged. This is a fantastic, challenging job. I think there could be people ready to pay to do it." He smiled, and asked: "Are you going to pay for it?" I laughed, answering: "For the time being I would rather get a salary for it."

It is not an exaggeration that you should have that feeling. Being a CEO is not just a job. You must make it personal to deliver at your best. The power behind your actions should come from your heart and your strongest values.

I was arguing with some colleagues a few years ago about the issues generated by a new supplier who was not delivering on time. It was affecting our ability to take to market an innovative solution that was in high demand. I was really frustrated and upset because we were letting down some of our best customers. One of my colleagues said: "Luis, don't feel so bad. Don't take it personally." I answered: "For me, this is personal." It was not just a task; our ability to provide a high level of service to our customers was at risk. I was ready to bring my passion for the business to revert the situation.

II.I.e BALANCED

I found the CEO job incredibly intellectually demanding. But it is also demanding physically and emotionally. It means that you must reach a fine balance between all the aspects of your life. Mind, body and soul should be taken care of.

We only have one life. So, when people talk about work-life balance, there is a risk that they think they are not living when they work. Work is an integral part of your life, and in this kind of job it is a large proportion of your time. In fact, it is most of your time. In mentoring conversations, I always recommend my mentees to take an integrated perspective of their time. In their lives, there should be space for work, for family, for friends, and for themselves. How much space you allocate to each will vary, depending on what stage you are at. For me, it can be very frustrating to consider work as the opposite to life. It requires a mature approach to balance your time well. But you are one individual, living several experiences which should enrich each other.

To be balanced, you need to find your sources of energy as well. My family is one of my best foundations. My wife and my four children give me the support and challenge I need. They are ready to help and discuss ideas or concerns. They are also prepared to push back if they think I am wrong. That gives me an incredible amount of energy when facing new adventures.

One day, I was nominated 'Telecommunications Engineer of the Year'. I came home excited and proud, and I couldn't wait to tell my family. One of my kids asked: "Dad, are you the best of all engineers?" "Only of telecommunications," I answered. "Dad, are you the best of all telecommunications engineers in the world?" "Only in Spain," I said. "Well, it is still very good," he concluded. He kept my feet on the ground.

I remember a colleague talking about his frustrations about not spending enough time with his kids, and that they did not share anything about their school or their friends with him. My answer was that it is not only about the amount of time, it is also about the quality of it. I asked him if he was sharing anything about his activity at work. If you tell your family what you do and how you feel about it, it is more likely that they will feel happy about disclosing their own lives. My children, and of course my wife, have always followed what I was up to at work. Even when they were very young, I explained the main products and solutions we were proud of, and why I was excited about it. Somehow, my kids expressed their own feelings and stories from their school or sports in return.

Meeting people, employees or customers, is another essential source of energy for me. I learn something new from every conversation, which is refreshing and inspiring.

Travelling, packed agendas and business meals are not the best of friends when it comes to your health. To deal with the CEO job you must be fit. You should learn how your body works, the effects of different foods, the importance of glucose levels and eating five times a day. Exercise will open your mind as well as improving energy levels and reducing health risks. Make sure you make time for your body, in whichever form you decide. A healthier approach will make you a stronger and more effective leader.

I started running a few years ago. At the beginning I found it boring and difficult. But over time I started to enjoy it. Distances were longer, routes were diverse and I found I could think or reflect on topics in a different way. I also used the time to listen to music or learn a new language. Those running moments became special opportunities to be with myself. A bubble in which I challenged myself to make a better time, or vary it with some high-intensity training to complement the set of workouts. You should find the best way to care for your body and enjoy it.

Busy agendas leave you with small amounts of time to free your brain. So, you should find ways of moving away from thinking about your business. Liberating your mind will help you to take stock and build fresh approaches to open questions or issues. You can do this in many ways – a hobby, family time, reading novels or any other method. Find the one that works best for you. You need it, and don't just leave it for the summer break as we usually do.

Personally, I enjoy doing Sudoku with a limited time frame. So, whenever I fly, I wait until the seatbelt sign is switched on and challenge myself to finish them before landing. It is a simple way of forcing my brain to do a different exercise. Lately, I have started to learn to play the piano, an incredibly difficult task for me which requires my full attention. It is great for developing other areas of the brain.

To get an integrated balance, you must also consider how you take care of your soul. The spiritual part is an even more personal one. I have found that Asian cultures manage this much better than in Western areas. I do recommend you start practising whatever you think would fit better for you. I do meditation when I feel stressed. I found that by doing it you get a better balance in peace of mind, happiness and calm. It has helped me to deal with difficult moments and enjoy the good ones more.

II.II ENGAGEMENT DIMENSION. YOUR CONNECTION SKILLS

The engagement dimension is the one you use to build connections with the outside world. These skills are the ones that helped me create strong, valuable relationships. They are the foundation for communicating, taking people with you, learning, and constructing a robust network of associations. You should be inspiring, a curious listener, humble to learn, empathetic, and connected to the world.

II.II.a INSPIRING

I have experienced the importance of taking the time to inspire people. As a CEO, especially with the combined Evangelist and Engagement dimensions, you must be able to inspire all kinds of stakeholders – not just in what you say but also in how you act. The shadow you cast is larger than you think. So, inspiration can be driven as much, or even more, with what you do as with what you say.

Being inspiring in your communications should be an objective. Not everybody is a natural communicator. It means that, as with any other CEO skill, it can be learned, trained or developed. Don't be shy to ask for help. There is no better improvisation than the one you have rehearsed five times. It means you care about the audience and you are willing to spend the time on it to provoke a deeper impact.

I learned that when you want to communicate with a large team, this is even more important as there are fewer opportunities to interact with them. When I was a CEO, we had over 20,000 people in 62 countries. To make the most of each chance to speak to them, I spent a good amount of time preparing. I used mind maps as a way of visualising all the messages I wanted to land. I worked closely with the internal communications team who supported me, discussing the tone, the main messages, and what we expected as the outcome of each video or audio call. Good preparation will mean a better delivery of an inspirational message. Make sure you spend quality time on preparation.

When it comes to inspiring people, there is a 'what' and a 'how'. Clear messages which speak to both the intellectual and emotional sides of your audience are more impactful than purely factual ones. However, the way you deliver them can also make a big difference.

When we were conducting a major restructuring of the company, we wanted to make sure that our people were involved. The internal communications team suggested taking a storytelling approach to explain the whole plan, why it was happening, the outcome we expected, and why the role of each person was important. It was key to get the personal engagement of the team around the world. We called the programme 'The difference is you'. We organised over 250 events across our operations. Nearly all our employees went through it, and they participated actively. We made sure that members of the leadership team were present at each event. It became a set of inspirational opportunities.

II.II.b CURIOUS LISTENER

The CEO must be an active listener. The best way to learn about the business, and get feedback from customers and your people, is by having conversations in which you spend more time on the receiving side. My grandmother told me: "You have two eyes, two ears and one mouth. Use them proportionately." As a business leader, I have struggled with it. I like to tell. I have strong opinions based on the knowledge I have acquired over years of experience. So, I find it easier to share it. People would expect the CEO to do so. However, if you are not careful you risk missing the other part of the world's knowledge and experience: that which you don't have.

On several occasions, I have found myself speaking too much. In one breakfast event with a team in the north of England, I was in a round table event, sharing my perspective of the business and how technology was changing our operations. In the last five minutes, when I stopped and allowed time for comments, I felt embarrassed. The team started to make extremely good points. I realised I had missed an opportunity by not letting them share their thoughts, concerns and ideas. Starting with their suggestions, and building on them, would have been better. I learned a lesson.

Curiosity is a very useful power when it comes to customers. Being curious means asking about their business, their sector trends and their strategy. Being ready to ask and listen actively could become a powerful selling tool. Sincere curiosity will also increase your knowledge about the world. Developing an inquisitive attitude will get you deeper when analysing problems as well.

I learned that asking questions complements your natural inclination to provide direction and guidelines. It makes people think, get involved and become part of the solution process.

II.II.c HUMBLE TO LEARN

To be a CEO you will need a big ego. By that I mean that you need a lot of confidence in yourself. You must understand and believe in your strengths and capabilities. However, you should also develop the power of being humble. I learned it when I took my first management role, even before I turned 30. I had high expectations of myself and was probably even overconfident. However, there was a big organisation change, I was moved to a different job and I had to start almost from scratch. It made me reconsider my core capabilities.

Being humble means also being open to changing your mind. It means you acknowledge that others may know more than you, and that even if they think differently from you, they can be right. Having strong opinions as a CEO and making them explicit is normal. Leaving space to be challenged is essential to making better decisions. It means slowing down your reaction and not jumping to conclusions too quickly.

Displaying humility, recognising that you still have more to learn, will help to drive the same behaviour across the organisation. You can create a learning culture by being open to acquiring new knowledge and expertise.

You must also be ready to keep learning through several sources. Over the years, I have built a list of publications, online magazines and Twitter feeds that I use as my sources of information. I read articles, watch videos, follow authors, and share some of that news with my team. A few of them are well-established journals, but others are alternative media or places where you find less standard news. It saved me time and facilitated a level of awareness that I found indispensable.

II.II.d EMPATHETIC

I believe that a great CEO should allow people to know him. A leader who is close to the team would gain their support more easily than a distant one. To create empathy, link into what motivates people. I always tried to understand their personal context and their professional ambitions. Aligning company objectives with their personal aspirations will facilitate their achievement. You can act as the bridge between both.

You must be open to being exposed. Being vulnerable will facilitate the connection with people. They want to know the person behind the job.

A team manager asked to have the CEO in one of her team meetings so that they could connect better with senior management. The session was quite tense to start with as they had planned to ask tough questions about the lack of resources, complicated communications, and getting a smaller reward than they believed they deserved, given their high performance. As the CEO, I asked them about their challenges and shared my own difficulties openly. For example, one person raised that they did not like long, complicated communications, stating they would prefer short messages. But their colleague spoke up and said that, in fact, they valued the longer, content-rich messages. Even in the room you could see the discrepancies, and I explained my own difficulty in trying to tailor communications to different people with different preferences.

While there was no right answer, the team appreciated the opportunity to have the conversation, and came away with a greater understanding, not just of the reasons behind their frustrations but also of the challenges of my own role as CEO. We moved on to a more personal conversation, and I shared stories about my family and my personal interests. For them, it was an opportunity to know the man behind the job – and it worked. In the next employee engagement survey, the team's perception of senior management improved more than 20%.

Empathy is created mainly in informal moments, conversations in which the human side of the CEO can be seen. Those occasions are also memorable for people.

When I was with one of the sales specialists, he told me about something that had stayed in his memory. He told me that, a few years before, he had been preparing an offer for a large customer. I passed by his desk and stopped to ask him what he was working on. He expressed how grateful he was for the significant amount of time I spent with him, discussing the deal and making suggestions how to improve it. Those moments create empathy with your team.

The same applies to customers. Whether it is the big things, such as when they face an issue in their operations and you offer to help, or the small things, such as remembering when they celebrate an anniversary as a company. These things will help you to develop a relationship beyond any commercial arrangement or contract.

An earthquake in South America had a big impact on a customer. They had problems contacting their people and their factories, and they were unable to serve their own customers. We reached out and offered them our support. We recovered some communications through satellite links, which helped employees to contact their families and perform some basic business activities that were critical for them. A few weeks later, I had a conversation with their local management. They were incredibly grateful for the quick and generous response, praising our team and their willingness to help. They said they would never forget it.

II.II.e CONNECTED

Being connected to the outside world is necessary to keep your feet on the ground. I think it is also the best opportunity to get visibility as a leader and support the company objectives. You should develop your network of relationships throughout your career. Keeping regular contact, and following the different paths people take, is the best way to build a great business and personal community – your community of connections.

The first time I met Keith Ferrazi, author of *Never Eat Alone,* we discussed the importance of networking. His work supporting sales teams over several years had reassured him of the power of a solid set of relationships. Every conversation is an opportunity to connect with someone and pick up additional knowledge and experience. It is also another potential chance for business or support in the future. The extended use of social business networks is helping me to stay in touch and even create new connections. But the real art is in sustaining them. I have enjoyed keeping those contacts as we follow each other through our careers.

Being connected externally provides the chance to create thought leadership and become a recognised leader. You can develop a personal brand, or serve as a figurehead for your company.

I took a mixed approach. You should not share or publish any opinions that conflict with those of your company. I have been very careful whenever I published any content. As a CEO, there is no such thing as a 'personal opinion'. However, there are articles, views or news that, when shared, could make you an influencer in the market. For example, I published a number of blogs in my name, supported by my company, as part of the World Economic Forum. In one particular blog, I asked whether a robot could replace a CEO. Considering the increased penetration of artificial intelligence, it was a provoking question, and my conclusion was that there are a growing number of assistance tools for CEOs to take more informed decisions and become more efficient. But the article triggered some good conversations and helped to raise my reputation.

The final area in which you should be connected is to the reality of society. People with economic and social challenges cannot be forgotten. You should stay connected to non-profit organisations and see how you can contribute. The visibility of your role will inspire others if you are truly committed, or if you facilitate others to do volunteering or to raise funds for good causes. You can make a difference from your position.

For example, The Prince's Trust activity is incredibly inspiring for me. Their programmes to integrate disadvantaged young people, helping them to recover their confidence and enter the job market, are remarkable. I had the opportunity to attend several of their events, and for four years I led a team to cycle in their annual Palace to Palace ride. From Buckingham Palace to Windsor Castle, we met teams from many different companies who were taking part to raise money for such a motivating cause. It was a great personal experience, especially the last one, as three of my children joined me. They were of a similar age to those the charity supports. I realised just how privileged we are, and how easy it is to forget it.

II.III EXECUTION DIMENSION. YOUR EXECUTION SKILLS

I always find the strongest sense of achievement is associated with the delivery of results. The Execution dimension is the most pragmatic and results oriented. These skills are the ones that you will use to drive high performance. They will be the foundations of your ability to deliver and to generate the outcomes you aim for. You should be focused and disciplined, bold in your decisions, unreasonable in your demands, entrepreneurial in your perspectives and resilient to confront challenges.

II.III.a FOCUSED

I found that time is one of your most scarce resources. It means that managing your agenda and your schedule well will become a differentiator in your success, and your assistant will be a key factor. The way you work with him or her will determine your productivity, to some extent. By creating an efficient team, you will save time and respond more effectively to your emails, prepare meetings and drive better outcomes. I did it, for example, by constantly asking: "What is this meeting for?" I also made sure that my office steered others on how I preferred to deal with information – the kind of customer briefings that worked best for me, or how to keep me informed about issues. Your office can also establish priorities for meetings, and arrange conversations in advance of other critical events. It allowed me to have more time to be focused on core topics.

You can make your team's lives easier and drive higher efficiency by being disciplined, not only on the topics but also on how to organise and run meetings. If you are not focused and disciplined, you can generate chaos around you and have a negative multiplier effect on the organisation.

We used to dedicate one day a week to meetings about service and transformation, with pre-populated agendas. Presenters had to send documents in advance to facilitate pre-reading, and focus the session on the discussion. We kept a register of actions that had been agreed so that it was easy to follow them. I found it essential to keep such discipline.

The large variety of topics that pass by your desk means you need to switch frequently from subject to subject. Being able to do this in a matter of seconds is a capability that I had to develop. Once I have moved to the next discussion, I must be focused on it; I could not leave my mind behind on the previous one.

To be focused requires that you also decide which data you will use to take decisions. You will need to discern which information is relevant, and which is accessory. Time is of the essence, so focused and high-quality data is critical for you.

In one discussion with a HR leader from a consulting firm about relevant data, I came across one of those examples of useless information. We were debating which data was needed to do effective comparisons between regions. She told me that in one company there was a robust discussion about salaries. One data item they had considered was the company's average salary per employee. They quickly realised that it was not meaningful, because market conditions in different countries are very varied – compare Germany and India, for example. It is worth dedicating time to making sure you focus on relevant data.

The areas of focus will also vary during the year depending on the budget cycle or customer big deals. They will also change based on your situation.

When I was leaving BT, I focused on the departure plan and created a 'last 30 days' plan, which comprised working with my successor, managing customer messages, talking to the team, and providing updates on critical projects. Keeping the focus during your exit period ensures a smooth transition. It reassures your team, your customers and all stakeholders, and builds a good foundation for the next phase of the project you were leading.

II.III.b BOLD

Making decisions is one of your privileges as CEO. I felt a strong responsibility to do it in the best possible way. You must choose sensible inputs, and facilitate time for discussion. However, you should be decisive. Sometimes you will need to opt for alternatives that might be less obvious, or options that do not have the full consensus of the team. I sometimes had to make it clear that, as a CEO, I was not leading a democracy. The task is to make sure that there is a time for debate. Then, make a decision so that the team can move on to execution.

Many years ago, I was discussing with our legal counsel about a response to a public tender and why we should present an offer at a certain price. It was a difficult decision to make. He gave me the facts based on previous projects, but he did not feel comfortable giving a clear recommendation, given the risks involved. I could tell that he felt it would be safer not to make an offer, but I thought it was a risk we should take. It was a bold decision. We won the deal and it became the basis for a successful public sector business.

II.III.c UNREASONABLE

The CEO should generate a healthy demanding environment. Sometimes, some requests may seem unreasonable at first glance. However, pursuing them can result in dramatically improved performance. The CEO should develop a methodology and an instinct to drive demanding but fair targets.

The power of being unreasonable can produce a culture of high ambition. But if actual objectives are truly unachievable, it could end in disengagement.

I have learned, however, that people and organisations can perform better than they initially think. Sport is an inspiring field to look at. Many world records were responses to unreasonable demands. The lesson to learn here is that the demands were not set top down; the individual or the team set those unreasonable goals and worked together to achieve them. This is your job.

The task is not just asking for more; it is instilling in everyone that feeling and desire to go further. Satisfaction with results can always be complemented with the ambition to achieve more. It is important to get the right balance.

I got a good tip from a customer. He was the head of a service centre where they capture orders of new equipment from their own customers. In one of his team meetings, they reviewed the percentage of orders that were correct the first time they were input into the system. It was 93%. So, the team set the target of inputting 95% of orders right first time. He asked: "Why not 100%?" The actions the team would need to put in place would be the same, whether it was 95% or 100%: making sure the customer's address was correct, inputting the exact configuration of equipment or precise prices. So why stop at 95%? Was he unreasonable? Maybe. But his challenge was right.

II.III.d ENTREPRENEUR

I deal a lot with entrepreneurs. This is why I am convinced that one of the skills to develop is an entrepreneurial mindset. It is highly complementary to the traditional corporate CEO profile.

This means you must be ready to take risks. Some could argue this is because entrepreneurs might have fewer assets at stake when they start. But in any case, it is a fact that risk appetite is different. You can build such profile and balance with a solid risk management practice. Good understanding of the risks you run will be an essential component of taking risks.

Being less risk averse should be compensated with a faster reaction when things go wrong, or when the market changes. Agility becomes a differentiator for the entrepreneurial CEO. It appears as a competitive advantage. Reading the market and acting quickly can secure entrance in new areas, or securing incremental business.

As the poet Gael Attal wrote: "A ship is safe in the harbour, but that's not what ships are built for." Keep this in mind when considering risk.

Other elements to develop under this power are intuition and readiness to innovate. You have a lot of knowledge, which creates a sixth sense of what is right. This is close to what an entrepreneur would do. Don't let your intuition get crushed by the accumulation of corporate data. And regarding innovation, it is also about being ready to stop and restart when it is needed.

After one holiday period, I decided to come back to the office as if I were new to the job. It was not an easy exercise. However, I decided to ask the questions a newcomer would ask, and question why things were done in a certain way. It triggered very good discussions, and we ended up stopping some things and accelerating others. It is your entrepreneurial side that can make those statements and challenge those established uses that are there 'because we always did it like that'.

II.III.e RESILIENT

There will always be difficult moments in your job. I believe that resilience is probably your most important power. As a leader, you will deal with uncertainty. Changing regulatory frameworks, new players entering the market, or political movements. This uncertainty will affect your team, who will look to you for certainty. You will not be able to provide it. But you will have to explain the situation and live with it.

One unexpected aspect of being a CEO, where you could struggle, is loneliness. You will face some decisions on your own. It could be when you are at a strategic crossroads, or when you must ask someone to leave the company. Even with allies and people you can trust, you will still be alone on many occasions. In those moments, you need to be resilient.

You will also face failure and defeat. You might be tempted to give up. Failure could be down to decisions you have made, or down to unexpected events. Setbacks can happen when you lose a deal you have put a lot of energy and time into. You might have fought hard and still lost. You will feel frustrated and angry. This is where your self-recovery skills play a critical role. Staying calm and looking ahead will be essential when it comes to keeping your team together in those storms.

We worked over several months on a competitive tender for an oil and gas company. The whole team were confident they would win. They worked long hours and weekends. It was an important reference in the market and the quality of the proposal was high. But we lost. The team were incredibly frustrated. Some said that we would never win business like this. They found it hard to work on such big deals for such a long period of time, running the risk of not winning. So the sales director and I went to the team to thank them for the hard work.

Despite the fact they didn't win, we would still be able to reuse their work in other tenders for other customers – their work was not wasted. We also went to see the customer, reassuring them that we would compete in future opportunities. They appreciated our gesture and arranged a session to explain why we lost. We used the session to learn, and continuing to spend time with the customer despite our loss put us in the best place for the next opportunity. Eighteen months later, we secured a significant piece of business with them, with an even stronger relationship with the customer.

Reflection

We have gone through the core skills needed to become a three-dimensional CEO. Mastering all of them will take time. However, it is good to reflect on which ones are your stronger, and in which ones you want to be better.

Rate yourself on a scale of 1 to 5 (5 being best in class) for each of the skills on where you think you are today. Do the same, in a different colour, where you want to be. Define the time frame in which you want to achieve that improvement. Set some actions you can measure and establish milestones to check your progress.

A visual way of doing it is by drawing a spider graph with the groups of five core skills that support each of the three dimensions.

Evangelist skills

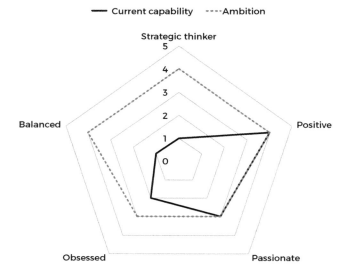

Engagement skills

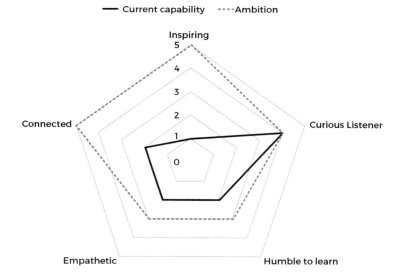

Execution skills

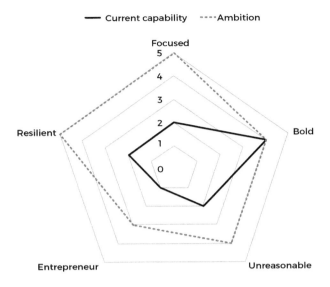

CHAPTER III

CREATE A VISION

There is no CEO without a vision. The first task of your Evangelist dimension is to create one using your strategic thinking capability. This means defining what you and your team want to achieve, making it memorable, connecting it with the emotions of the team, underpinning it with facts, and making sure it is relevant to the market in which you operate.

Once appointed as CEO, you ask yourself: so now what? There are books and articles about the question, but there is nothing specifically for you, your business and the circumstances around it at the exact moment you got the job. The expectations from the board, the market and even your people are not always clearly defined. Everybody expects you to lead, making the business a better one, a superior organisation – whatever that might mean. For yourself, you want to make sure that when you leave the company it is remarkably better than when you started. You aim to be proud of leaving a legacy with an incremental value for all stakeholders: customers, employees, suppliers, shareholders and society.

Define what you want to achieve

So, the first challenge is to make it clear: what do you want to achieve? What is the destination for the organisation you are starting to run? What is the vision? How will you create this vision, which will be the foundation for the execution plans to make it happen? A well-articulated vision is key, so that you can check it with your key stakeholders, making sure you match expectations and avoid misunderstandings later down the line. It will be the basis for the long-term sustainability of the business.

A longer term vision is not easy to have. In 2010 I went to India and spent 10 days in different cities. We met big companies, government bodies, small organisations. We also spent time with non-government organisations, like one supporting 'street kids', as well as with a lot of people from the technology industry.

One of my best takeaways from that trip came out of a chat with the dean of the Indian Institute of Technology in Bengaluru (Bangalore at the time). His reflection was: "You have to define what you want to be famous for. We have chosen a few areas where we would like to be best in class in 2020. For example, in India, water treatment is essential for our citizens. To be best in the world in 10 years, we must start now. We are recruiting the best experts in the world. We are creating an ecosystem of relationships with large companies and government funds that will help entrepreneurs in the field, and we are creating a new stream of studies with deep research about water treatment. It is a collective decision across business, government, society and university to deal with water treatment and make it a subject of leading expertise. If you don't define what you want to be the best at, you don't plan, you don't execute with others, and it will never happen. It is like a sportsman who wants to be best but does not decide in which sport."

It made me think. Since then, I have tried to understand in which areas we were aiming to be famous for, and then align investments, talent recruitment and long-term focus behind it. This is the core of the vision you should build.

The vision should also respond to a set of key questions that any organisation should be prepared to answer:

"Why do we exist?" That is the mission. "What do we want to be?" That is the vision. "How do we aim to get there?" That is the strategy with the associated focus on implementation.

Then, you should be ready to keep responding. "How you will measure the progress?" That is your dashboard or balance scorecard. "What does each unit have to do?" Your operational plans. "What does each individual have to do?" Personal plans. And all of that is underpinned by the values: "What do we stand for?" This is the architecture of your business. Having clear answers will make it possible for everybody to contribute and get engaged with the organisation's objectives.

Articulate the vision

The next step is: how do you create or define that vision? The vision is a long-lasting description of what you aspire to be as a business. It is important to articulate the vision so that you can share it and use it to inspire others, making them part of it.

When I was appointed CEO, we spent a few weeks defining the vision for the business. We used a good number of conversations with different stakeholders, aiming to have a complete vision built together. It was key to include the key components of our business in that vision.

The first component was the income: the revenue coming in from products and services. Our aim was to make sure we focused the organisation on growing our core customers and products, even if other areas were declining. We wanted to be a growing business.

The second component was, like every company, the cost base. Costs are neither good nor bad; it is the efficiency that counts. The cost per produced unit is more important than the overall amount of cost. So, we wanted to be getting more efficient every day.

The third component was the very essence of our business: to provide service; to act as an extension of the customer's operations. Happy customers buy more. So, we wanted to have customers who love to work with us.

Finally, our ambition was for our team to be a key differentiator. We wanted to create a team that was ready to go the extra mile to support a customer. A team that could feel the importance of their job – for the company, for our customers and for the society. We wanted to have people who felt proud to be making a difference.

We called it 'the next generation of Global Services'. The vision was to create a growing business which was getting more efficient every day, with customers who love to work with us and people who were proud to make a difference. Four key elements of a vision: growth, profit, customer service, and people engagement, and we defined the associated targets to each category.

Once you have defined it, it is key to validate it with your stakeholders. It could be the CEO of the group if you are a divisional or regional CEO, or the board. Either way, you must gain that active confirmation. Why? Because it will be the reference to come back to when discrepancies or challenges appear.

The analyst community is also important to bring on board. The vision should be compelling for them, whether they're industry experts that customers use as a reference to make decisions, or financial analysts who make recommendations about investments. Scheduling time with them will be a key part of the CEO role.

As such, your role as Chief Evangelist Officer is to enable the creation of the vision, share it across and outside of the organisation, and define the framework to make the execution possible. That Evangelist dimension of the leader will create something unique to inspire others, a vision that can mobilise the rest.

Bring together your organisation around an image

The vision is not something to be kept on a shelf. Successful organisations put their vision at the core of everything they do. When you start sharing it, your ambition is to make it memorable for the team. We all know that an image is worth more than a thousand words. So, the question is how to associate that vision with something unforgettable for people, linking it to something most people can relate to. The challenge is making sure that everybody can identify himself or herself with the vision, winning over hearts as well as minds. I found that the best way is through powerful images.

Make sure you pick an inspiring image or project name. Make it real, a challenging but possible reference, and keep the consistency when using it. The impact will be higher if the image is associated with something difficult to achieve, but that someone has accomplished. To some extent, someone who has made the impossible possible.

This powerful image will become part of your daily conversations and meetings, and it should be the container for the targets and plans to execute the vision. Some people use acronyms or key words. There is no rule here; however, make sure they trigger inspiring thoughts and feelings.

When I was CEO of the Spanish business, we planned for a multiyear project to improve the profitability of the operation. We aimed to inspire people without hiding the challenge and difficulty of doing it. We came up with the name 'Aconcagua', the highest peak in the Andes mountains. It is one of the 8K Peaks (14 peaks over 8,000 metres) that any great mountaineer dreams of conquering. We chose it because to attack such an objective means a lot of preparation and planning. You need food specialists, telecommunications experts and health professionals. You need to understand the weather, know different routes to follow, and have an exit plan B in case of emergency.

For such an adventure, you need a solid financial plan and a good cost analysis, and of course, the right equipment in terms of clothes, tents, boots and sleeping bags. Finally, the physical and mental preparation of the team is key. They must resist the fatigue and be prepared to deal with different levels of oxygen and pain. They also need the mental resilience to continue when their body is screaming: "No more." They need the mindset to keep going, not just for them but also to support the rest of the team.

Those were the reasons why we picked Aconcagua – a challenging journey that needed a lot of resilience and focus. And we launched it.

Everybody in the team started to refer to Aconcagua. We put up posters with drawings of the mountain and the different roles, and we defined clear targets. We brought an alpinist who had climbed it to one of our employee events. I have never seen such level of commitment in a team. Aconcagua became, in effect, a 'business as usual' name. It helped to review, confirm or cancel plans. It made sure we kept the focus on improvements to our customer service and our levels of efficiency. After two years, we accomplished most of the plan. It was very difficult at times and we often had the feeling that it would not happen. However, we learned a lot. Not just about our business and our customers, but also about us as individuals and as a team.

In summary, an important addition to a clear description of the vision could be a powerful image that people can relate to. Sometimes, a vision with a set of objectives could be too abstract and far from what people can recognise from the 'real world'. A vision could be a long-term ambition, and you might need to achieve some intermediate steps. You can focus on a subset of well-defined milestones with this approach. I also learned that the more real those images or projects can be, the better. Align this image with a clear set of targets, track them, share how they progress, and you will have the whole team behind you.

Drive consistency

Once you have identified the image or name, and clarified its ambitions, there is one key word: consistency. Normally, these programmes have a two to three year time frame. It takes time to internalise and connect the vision with the image. That is why, once you have decided on it, consistent communication is key. 'Boringly consistent' is, in general, a good approach when you want a message to go through an organisation.

Mobilise cathedral builders

A strong and clear vision will make it easier to make the right decisions. It will make sure you keep the focus of the whole organisation. It will avoid wasting time and effort on the wrong things. By having a vision and a powerful image, you might gain the intellect and the emotional connection of everyone. It is a very difficult task and occasionally it could even be frustrating. But when an organisation manages to have all its employees fully aligned along the vision, it becomes unbeatable. It is worth the effort.

When it comes to describing the way you would like your team to share a vision, and link to the individual's pride, one of my favourite stories is the 'cathedral' story. You might have heard it.

The story is about a man who walks past a construction site. As he approaches, he notices two individuals doing the same job. They are taking bricks from a big pile, applying mortar, and putting them on top of each other to make a wall. As he gets closer, he notices that whilst one is doing a good, efficient job, the other stops briefly after placing each brick, makes sure it is well secured, before starting on the next one. The man was intrigued and approached the workmen. He asked the first one what he was doing. With an expression of surprise, he looked at the man and said, with his hands open towards the wall: "I am putting bricks and mortar together. Can't you see?" "Thank you," said the man. He kept walking and asked the same question to the second workman. The workman stopped a second and looked at him. He looked at the wall and above it, and said proudly: "I am building a cathedral."

This is what every organisation needs – 'cathedral builders'. Not everybody can be the architect or the designer, but everybody can be a 'cathedral builder'. The second workman in the story knew the purpose of his job. But even more importantly, that sense of direction and vision made him both proud and responsible. He knew his wall was going to be part of an important monument. So, he wanted the wall to be in line with such an inspirational building. He did not want to do a poor job. Clearly, someone inspired him – the architect or the construction manager took the time to explain what kind of building they were making, and why his job was so important. But, at the end of the day, it will be the personal attitude that will make the difference to the outcome of the cathedral.

How we applied the story

We had embarked upon a large transformation of our division. We had the objective of consolidating our leadership in the market, and achieving an improved financial performance. As with any big venture, you need as many people as possible to fully embrace it.

We were sharing the transformational plan with the 120 most senior managers in our division, and we decided to build on the 'cathedral' story. We wanted to make sure everybody felt part of, and core to, the construction of a better business.

We started the meeting by telling the story and explaining why it was relevant to us. The business we were aiming to build was comparable to the cathedral once finished. We already had the existing foundations of the business: a solid customer base, a good portfolio, well-reputed service and a skilled and dedicated team around the globe. But this was just the base.

After sharing the actual plans behind each of the four business drivers, we wanted to have the emotional buy-in to execute against them.

We offered the opportunity to decide whether or not to be part of building 'the cathedral' by walking to the stage, taking a brick and putting it in a 'wall' we had constructed. Then someone suggested that the real way to show personal commitment was to sign the bricks. And it happened. Our senior managers signed those bricks and they remained in my office until I left the business.

This story went viral quickly and I started to receive in my office signed bricks from all over the world – including Brazil, Argentina and Singapore. In Germany, they prepared a website where you could print your own paper brick and fold it. Our financial market team wanted to mix the cathedral 'theme' with the traditional stock exchange bells, so they brought in a beautiful bronze bell. In the US, when I went to Dallas, the team started to build a wall with a brick for each deal they had won. They could proudly see, at the entrance of their offices, the progress they were making and the contribution from everyone. More importantly, the cathedral theme represented a way of unifying the message, representing a joint ambition to build something together.

Connect with dispersed teams

As a CEO, your messages must reach the whole company. Large global organisations face a big challenge when they try to connect with geographically dispersed teams. I had the opportunity to run a team of more than 20,000 people across 62 countries. Landing the vision message, even using powerful images, was a challenge. Technology provides new ways of reducing physical distance, but there is never as solid a connection as when you meet face-to-face. Your role is making sure the leadership presence is felt in those remote parts.

When you are planning visits and meetings, localising the message is a key component to making an impact. For dispersed teams, it is easy to get isolated, and the feel they get from their company can be very different from how teams feel 'in the centre'. However, customers meet our global teams in several locations and expect to get the same experience of solutions, service and values each time, wherever they are. So, addressing dispersed teams is essential to make sure that the vision and its associated objectives reach everyone.

When I was in banking, I had the chance to spend time with the CEO of a large Spanish bank. We were debating how technology was impacting the way we deal with customers, and how it improves operations. We discussed the importance of consistency, and I asked what was his biggest challenge as CEO. He said: "The most difficult thing is implementing the latest policy or product in every branch. It is a challenge to reduce the time from issuing instructions centrally to executing them locally. Sometimes it takes even months for a new procedure to be used in a small remote branch. Technology can help, but behaviour is key."

Then he explained how he had been taking reports from the IT systems directly when visiting a branch. Word got out and his visits went viral. Suddenly, everyone started to pay attention to the newest orders and processes, and reduced the implementation time as a result.

I have remembered this story all these years, and I had a similar challenge as CEO. It is difficult for a team in a Buenos Aires data centre to feel and capture the same spirit of the message as a team in Durban in South Africa. That consistency and discipline makes a difference. It must start with clarity from the top, combined with a rigorous cascade process, and if you want to have everybody aligned behind the vision, you must remember distant teams.

Make the vision real

Once a vision exists and the basic emotional connection is there, it is necessary to underpin the vision with facts. There are three elements to consider: defining tangible results, providing tools to facilitate the spreading of the message, and connecting to the day-to-day jobs of your employees.

Remember the importance of defining clear targets for the whole organisation. They keep the focus and keep everybody aligned to the vision. If the vision is clear, and the associated images are inspiring, then the targets would be the final complement needed to set the base for the value creation you aim to accomplish.

Support your people managers

Providing tools to help managers is another important component. The role of the immediate line manager becomes critical when you deal with teams that are in different locations or units that do a variety of jobs. Those managers are responsible for landing the vision and making it relevant to each team, and to each individual. As I mentioned earlier, consistency is essential, and you often need tools to reinforce it. I have learned that you need to accompany the vision message with user guides that provide the detail behind it. They will make it easier to spread the vision effectively around the globe.

When you have 3,000 managers in 60 countries, you would be mad to imagine that a centralised message sent from the CEO is going to land perfectly in every corner of the organisation. Sometimes, those managers don't have the knowledge or experience to share the message you wish everybody to get. In this case, it is just as important to make clear how everyone fits into the overall strategy. The individual job, what they do every day, and how they are part of the bigger picture is an association you must help to build. This is where the connection between the Evangelist and the Engagement dimensions of the leader is key.

In our case, we decided to create what we called a Playbook. Initially, it was a collection of PowerPoint slides, which included a few questions to make it easier for a manager to follow with his team, helping them to fully understand the implications of the contents. We thought carefully about how to make sure the different functions could understand the impact they have on the joint ambition. The manager's role was, then, to make it relevant to their team by using stories they can link to their day-to-day job, so that they would recognise their contribution to the bigger picture. Those sessions generated feedback, ideas and questions that helped to refine what we wanted to do and how we were going to do it. We ended up with a fully interactive version, with video content and chat options. It fostered collaboration and a better reach of the message.

Between them, our managers held over 2,400 sessions, touching all our employees around the globe. They captured feedback on how to clarify certain areas, make them more relevant or adjust the content to specific markets. As a result, we saw an 18% improvement in a very specific question in the employee engagement survey: 'Do you know the strategy?' It was a concerted effort from all the leaders in the business.

Co-create the vision with the market

The final aspect to consider when creating the vision is that you should continuously check it with the market. You would have built it using your strategic thinking skill. Now, you must contrast with others the validity of the vision. You have already done this with internal stakeholders; you must complement this with the external ones. They will be critical in the implementation phase. The vision should get the same buy-in from different communities that work with your organisation. Customers, analysts and suppliers must understand your vision, and make it theirs, in order to maximise its success. A vision that is not recognised by the market has a smaller opportunity to be successful. To do this, you must have a unique approach, you must have taken a degree of co-creation with your customers, and you should be open to being challenged.

A key question I used to ask myself when looking at the external side of the vision was: Why my company? Regardless of the business you are in, it is always important to ask yourself why customers would decide to buy from you. Competition is increasing in every sector, and through new technologies disruption is accelerating. So, the speed at which you must validate and understand your proposition to the market is critical. Knowing your unique selling proposition (USP) also helps to focus internal efforts and investments. It becomes the cornerstone to delivering the vision.

The best way to understand this USP is through customer conversations. In a business-to-business environment, there is nothing better than face-to-face discussions. In a retail business, there are other methods, such as using focus groups. In any case, incorporating the voice of the customer in your vision will make it a more compelling one and increase its chances of success.

When it comes to including the voice of the customer, there are some questions you must answer, such as: What is your portfolio vision? What services will make you relevant to customers?

I also questioned myself: What should my role be in this? Can a CEO help to create that portfolio vision?

I find it quite interesting to look at the very different profiles and skills of CEOs, and how they can make a difference. There is always a complement they must find in the rest of the team. The CEO can be the first sales executive, the main product designer, the super CFO or the leading operational guy, based on his experience. In fact, I learned that a leader should change 'hats' across the three dimensions. Even if his main skill is based upon a strong financial background, he should deploy his best sales skills in front of customers. I am an engineer, so personally I loved to be involved in creating new portfolio solutions and services.

As part of that process, you discuss with your team, your customers and your suppliers about the market – what trends are coming, and how should you face them? This was the basis for how one of the most compelling portfolio visions was created. It is how the 'Cloud of Clouds' was born.

I met with the CIO of a large manufacturing company in my office. We talked about his business: a technology company that works with top players, designing and manufacturing high-tech equipment. They have factories around the globe and a strong need to have their teams connected and collaborating.

He asked about our vision, and wanted me to describe where we were investing and the trends we saw in the market. A customer conversation is always a unique opportunity for a CEO. I decided to start drawing.

At the core of what we do for our customers is the network. So I drew five boxes to show the core equipment, and drew lines connecting them all to show their links – this constitutes the core of the network. (If you have seen the first drawing of Arpanet, the origin of the Internet, you would easily recognise this approach.) Connected to this network, we have our customers' offices, factories, data centres and other sites. In each of these, their employees – and, more and more, their devices – communicate using that infrastructure, sending digitised information. However, new solutions are supplied through what is called the Cloud. This means that services and applications are available over different infrastructures owned by multiple players. (As an ex-CIO, I knew the pressure to keep the agility and flexibility of your organisation while also keeping it secure, cost efficient, and performing at the highest possible level.)

The customer confirmed his vision of a multivendor environment complementing his own platforms: a hybrid Cloud. He needed a 'Cloud of Clouds'.

I kept drawing until we had the whole image of how we would respond to his challenges with our platforms. As the discussion progressed, we continued to refine the 'Cloud of Clouds' vision.

In the following days, we decided to test this draft vision with more customers and stakeholders. I presented it to the CIO of a mining company at the time, asking him to challenge and improve it, and we then presented it to the marketing and portfolio teams. Thanks to strong debates and constructive contributions from everyone, we continued to refine it.

I was surprised by the speed of responses from colleagues and customers alike, and delighted about the idea of co-creation. It showed me the true power of an organisation when it rallies around an idea, and how the mix of internal perspectives and customer demands can generate unique outcomes. The more we discussed Cloud of Clouds, the more we believed in it.

However, in any business there is always the risk of having too much support and not enough challenge. So we decided that before spending more valuable resources and time on it, we should test our vision further.

This is where you should be open to being challenged about what you think, or what you are executing.

Challenge the vision externally

At the headquarters of Gartner Group in the US, you find a quiet forest environment where you feel invited to think, reflect and conduct proper research. Meeting their CEO and a number of their analysts was inspiring. I explained to them that the objective of the session was to listen to their views and understand what we were missing, or where we may have gone wrong. I took them through the Cloud of Clouds over the following couple of hours, responding to their questions. They gave a solid market and customer perspective. They challenged how we would differentiate, and suggested that to keep consistency across all elements of the portfolio we should incorporate a solid security layer.

In the following months, we presented our thinking to other players, like Equinix, Huawei and Cisco. We discussed it with Google, Amazon and IBM. We engaged with Salesforce and some Fintechs. In every conversation, we learned where our value was, what we should improve, and why those leading players were ready to partner with us.

With this vision taking shape, we reviewed our investments in portfolio and infrastructure to make sure everything we were doing was to underpin Cloud of Clouds. Network investments, platform developments, systems improvements, monitoring and orchestrating tools – everything needed to serve the core strategy, and only the core strategy. We developed security platforms and adjusted them to support this open and flexible environment. We made sure that Professional Services would be able to help customers to navigate their journey into Cloud services. It was fascinating to see how a shared portfolio vision aligned such a large organisation. It affected all teams: sales learning how to explain it to customers, technical designers integrating services around Cloud platforms, and product managers aligning across portfolio lines.

But we were never complacent. We continued to ask the same questions: What is wrong with this? What are we missing? It was a step change in the way a telco's set of products and services were presented to the market. Very few companies can put their entire portfolio strategy into one diagram, one sheet of paper, in a comprehensive way that is easy to follow.

The team felt incredibly proud when industry analysts started to mention and recognise it. It became part of the company's presentations, and even competitors included it as one of the strategic trends.

This is probably one of the best experiences and achievements of my career: the co-creation of a portfolio vision that would last. It aligned an entire organisation, making them feel proud. It resonated with customers and the market recognised it as a differentiator.

Reflection

In this chapter, we have discussed the importance of developing a vision and how different core skills are used to do it. To reflect on it, consider the following questions:

- What is my vision for the business I run, or I am part of, in three or five years? What would I do differently?

- Can I explain my organisation's vision in a way that I get personally excited?

- Would I be able to share this with customers, my team and the market?

- Have they been involved in co-creating it?

- Can I explain it to my kids and make them feel proud of what I do?

If you are happy with the answers you have, well done. Then, make sure that your Evangelist dimension transforms everybody into a 'cathedral builder'.

CHAPTER IV

ENGAGE

E ngagement is the art of getting everybody to work together wholeheartedly towards a set of common goals that underpin the vision. It requires belief, pride and confidence to make it happen. It requires communicating relentlessly, listening as much as telling, connecting personally with all stakeholders and driving a positive energy across the whole organisation.

Communicate relentlessly

Communicate, communicate, communicate. This is a core task for the Chief Engagement Officer. The larger the team you lead, the more important the communication aspect is, to get the right levels of engagement. You will need many of your core skills – such as being inspiring, building empathy and actively listening. It is key to make sure that everybody aims to contribute in their job, executing their tasks with the highest quality and acting beyond their role descriptions to make a difference.

Define the message

When you communicate, you should be clear about the core messages you want to give, which channels of communication work best for your audience and finally, how to exploit each one in the best possible way.

Defining the message is the basis for proper communication. Although it seems obvious, I found that people are not always able to answer the simple question: What are you trying to achieve? What do you expect the audience to do as a result? Sharing a message for information, to publish news or keep people aware of what is happening, is OK. But it is unlikely to drive engagement. Your audience will read the news and learn about it, but if it is not clear how the news will affect the individual, the impact will disappear in minutes. Make sure that whenever you communicate, you know why you are doing it, what the core message is, and why the message is relevant to the audience.

The content of your messages can also include some basic principles or ideas you would like to use consistently. I decided to use three words when structuring my messages: gratitude, pride and confidence. Gratitude as a way of saying thank you for the effort people put into their jobs. Pride in what has been achieved, while also reflecting on what we were less proud of, and confidence in the future, using what we have learned to make our plans happen.

When it comes to communication, consider the scarcest resource we have: time. If people feel they are wasting their time when they read or watch your communications, regardless of the channel, you will lose them. So, make sure you think carefully what you want to say and why. It will save you time and it will increase the impact you will make. So, whether you are talking about customer wins, examples of brilliant service or financial performance, make it something that people can digest, remember and act on.

It is always useful for your support team to find out which topics people would like to hear more about. But make sure you don't communicate just what people want to hear. You are the owner of the message and you must make sure that it is clear, repeated relentlessly and understood everywhere.

Use storytelling

Telling a story helps to illustrate what you mean. I used to write a blog internally and, for example, I compared our business — and the importance of each role — to a business everybody is familiar with: a restaurant.

My restaurant

I have a great restaurant. We have a strong reputation among all gourmet experts. Even in the Michelin guide, we appear in the 'Best in the world' list. Our clients enjoy our food and our specialities. They keep coming back. Some of them have been coming to us for years; they have shared in our journey, and we have become part of their lives. They have celebrated anniversaries, birthdays and even made business negotiations at our tables.

Part of our success comes from the way we deal with our clients. Knowing that Mr Smith is vegetarian or that Mrs Piels has diabetes makes a real difference to them. Our clients' experience with us starts when they call us to book a table, and continues when they walk through the door and we recognise them and call them by their name. And finally, making sure we give them the right bill, and making sure they can pay by cash or card, is also important.

We often have an interesting debate about the menu. Do we offer our customers whatever they want? This would drive an unaffordable business. But having too limited a selection could make us less attractive to them. So it has to be 70/20/10. A very standard set of dishes (70%), a degree of flexibility (20%) such as the way meat is cooked or having salt-free dishes, and finally, an exceptional ability to offer bespoke meals (10%), such as plain omelettes for kids.

Making sure that our maîtres d'hôtel know the menu extremely well is also essential. We deliver proper training every morning to make sure they help our clients make the right decisions.

We also need to keep innovating, changing and adapting our menu,

---

according to the season. Our clients appreciate our innovation capabilities, which come from a profound knowledge of their tastes and the goods available in the market, as well as the management of kitchen technologies.

But sometimes we make mistakes: either we take an order with too many modifications, or we misunderstand a customer's order. This interface between our customer-facing team and our cooking team is key to achieving the best client experience. Making an error costs us a lot. We need to cook another whole meal for the customer, and their satisfaction goes down very quickly.

We have also faced significant challenges in the kitchen. At one point there were too many people there, making our kitchen too crowded to prepare food properly. Too many chefs create duplicate tasks, each one wanting to present the food in a different way, or even change the flavours. And having too many chefs can cost more than you can afford. A successful kitchen has the right number of people, clear directions from the chef, well-defined accountability and perfect execution.

Finally, it is impossible to have a great restaurant without proper food. Managing our suppliers is an art, getting high-quality food at the right price and understanding who the leaders in the market are.

This is why I am so proud of our restaurant. We know that being the best is hard work, and every day is almost like starting from scratch. But we cannot fail our clients. And we can only do this if we have the best people. Our maîtres d'hôtel, sommeliers, waiters, chef and cooks have to understand that our customers' experience is critical.

Our team could see the importance of supporting each other, and the relevance of every single job when it comes to delivering a great customer experience.

Choose the communication channels

Storytelling is a powerful technique that works well. It can tap into not only the intellectual side, but also, more importantly, the emotional side of your audience. It can be used in any communication channel. It can be done in face-to-face presentations, video or audio recordings, and even in writing.

When I took on my first large international role in July 2007, I started writing this internal blog. My responsibilities covered Europe, the Middle East, Africa and Latin America, with a direct team of over 8,000 people and many more supporting our customers from other business units. I thought to myself: how can we share what we are doing and what our principles are? How can we connect with our team in an interesting, easy-to-digest way?

Blogging offers you that opportunity. It does not need to happen regularly. It can be linked to real experiences, you can incorporate pictures (I became a selfie expert), it allows you to share thoughts, ideas and even feelings. It should be written simply. It also enables you to reach everybody. For non-native English-speaking people, the informal language is also easier to read. Finally, a blog must be personal. Nobody can or should write it for you. I blogged for 10 years, until the day I left the company. True, the quality was not always as good as the formal messages where I have had help. But it was fresh, it was me, and my audience appreciated the fact that it was genuine. It is demanding as well. If you decide to start a blog, you must be ready to keep going. There is always something to write about, to have an opinion on.

I was surprised by the reaction. I got a good number of followers. People would come up to me and talk about my last blog, or simply express their enjoyment of having a small window into what you do as a CEO. It is a very powerful complementary tool that can help to distribute key developments and messages in a more informal way.

A blog is just one channel. The Chief Engagement Officer should master all communication channels. In fact, the digital world in which we live has opened new channels. This is great, however it demands extra effort to coordinate and make good use of the capabilities of each one. As in any communication, it is key to think about the audience, and the channel that best connects you with them.

Different channels are useful for different purposes. Apart from the personal interactions and the blog, I used a variety.

I used email, mainly for one-to-one communication but also for small groups. It means you can personalise it, but it also requires short, sharp and focused communication. Ideally, it should be action oriented, as your audience is more likely to be engaged if they are directly involved. Which emails are you going to deal with personally, and which ones will your assistant manage? How will you use CC (copied to) or even BCC (blind copied)? Will your answers to messages trigger a chain of unnecessary responses? I don't need to go into detail about how to use email in the best possible way, but it is important to consider as your approach can affect your productivity.

I used the official newsletter channel in our business. This is best used for informative content, or 'news'. In our case, they were sent to everybody, but individuals could decide which news they wanted to receive so that it was relevant to them.

I enjoyed using social media – whether it was the internal, corporate tool for employees or external tools such as Twitter or LinkedIn. Social media gives you the opportunity to create and develop a personal brand. But doing so must be a conscious and considered decision. If you want to build a distinctive brand, it will require determination, attention and dedication. The content can be balanced between your industry knowledge and your personal reflections. If you do it well, you can become an industry reference or, as LinkedIn calls it, an influencer. The important thing is to understand that whatever is published internally or externally will be known in an open market – and sometimes, less is more. Retweeting for the sake of it will dilute your impact. I will only post when I believe I can add value.

Chatting is the most informal channel I have used, whether on an open consumer chat application or a chat tool embedded in a large corporate platform like Chatter within Salesforce.com. Chatting offers an agile way of discussing a topic, sharing information, posting questions or celebrating a new business deal. It can connect with one person or with a group of people. I found it valuable as an easy, quick, in-the-moment tool. Reacting to a customer issue, or getting an alert on key news, facilitates your personal efficiency. I loved it when a sales person would use a Chatter group to proudly share that an important contract had been signed.

The use of video is gaining traction as a communication channel, and it can take several forms. It can be a short video with a very focused message, or a longer video to discuss a specific topic in detail. Depending on the content, videos can be more easily consumed than written text, and they are more personal too. They can also go viral if you have good quality content. But they require even more preparation than any other channel or media.

We decided to record a video in which I explained the Cloud of Clouds portfolio vision, in the same way I would explain it to customers. We published it on YouTube and it became one of the most watched videos in the company's history. Why? Because it was not that common to have a CEO explain and draw the company's vision. It was a surprise, and surprises can work well in communication. It worked particularly well with customers and partners.

Events are one-off moments that take a significant amount of time out of your workforce – so they are your largest communication investment. It means that you should aim for the highest possible return. They can be face-to-face, or they can use technology-enabled channels such as video or audio conferences.

Online technology-based events, such as an hour-long video webcast discussing the last quarter's results and next quarter's priority areas, require good preparation and focus to capture and retain your audience's attention throughout. You will engage your audience through personal touches and a high quality of content. Always keep a slot for Q&A to make sure this type of communication is two-way.

Physical, face-to-face events represent the strongest opportunity for personal interaction. They are the highest investment of time and money because normally, on top of the time taken out for the event, you have additional costs including travel, catering and production.

Make events memorable

Given that events represent the largest investment and opportunity, let us look at them more closely. Internal events are a critical part of the way you communicate and engage within any organisation. Regardless of the size, geographical presence or type of business, a well-prepared internal event can make a difference. An event is not a just a large meeting; it can take the form of a conference with breakout sessions, or just one large presentation. The event can be for a core team of people or it can cover a vast population – in some cases, almost the whole company.

You should only organise an event if you know why you are doing it. Defining the objective is key. I have been to events in which I have asked myself why I was there. The answer 'well, this is the annual kick-off we always have' is not good enough. You need to be able to answer the key questions: How do you want people to feel and think when they leave? What actions or attitude do you expect in the days after?

Events deserve proper attention, planning and good execution. A well thought-through agenda can make a difference to the performance of the company. How many times have you heard: "This morning's sessions were good but the afternoon was boring and I have no idea what they wanted from us."? Having a strong, challenging team around you is the best way to get a high-quality agenda. This is a constant theme for a leader. Surround yourself with people who will tell you the truth, not just what you want to hear. That, combined with your personal engagement, will make an event something people will remember. Those moments are your moments of truth.

One year, we were launching the plan for a new fiscal year and we wanted to hold a global event. It was an annual event, so a rare opportunity that required excellent planning. We structured the event over two full days. Choosing the right venue was key. In the right place, you can create a warm team spirit. Being together in the right environment, working together, can make a difference.

We had a number of presentations from analysts and customers, to make sure we had the external reference.

But first, I started the event with an introduction. I invited members of the audience to share how they felt, share what was on their mind at that moment, and what they expected to get from the event. This is a great way to quickly judge the mood of the audience – excited, interested, tired or even sceptical.

During the break, we asked the most vocal people what they thought of the event so far. They said it was good to set the scene and to show the challenges, but we were not addressing the underlying blockers. We had not addressed the elephant in the room.

So, before going further with the planned agenda, we asked the audience about those blockers. What was stopping their plans? What are the taboos that weren't being discussed? We split the team into groups and asked them to write down those big issues. After 45 minutes of group discussions, we came back together. Those small teams shared their areas of concern and, there in the room, we either sourced an answer from the owner or a commitment to address it within a month.

If we had not discussed those underlying issues, the whole event would have been a waste of time. People would have been silently thinking about the blockers, and we would have been trying to deliver a message to a distracted disengaged audience.

In summary, I learned how team events offer three opportunities.

First, sharing the same clear message with the whole team at the same time. This has an intrinsic value because you make sure the communication is delivered in the way you want it. You also offer the opportunity to discuss clarifying questions and it also allows you to make the participants become part of the solution by engaging them in the conversation.

Second, fostering collaboration and networking within the team. People can influence the speed of processes. They can help colleagues. You can achieve something faster by encouraging people to pick up the phone and call a colleague, instead of just sending an email. It will be easier if they have met each other at the event.

Third, providing an external reference to make the event more relevant. It can be a sector expert who is disrupting your business, a brutal financial analyst, or customers explaining why they buy from you and outlining where they expect you to do better.

The challenge is how to build on those events afterwards – how to sustain the momentum you have generated in the space of a couple of days. You must also follow up on the actions. This will not only reinforce the value of the event but also set the basis for future events.

Identify and remove communication blockers

Well-defined messages and well-managed channels make your communication more effective. But there is always the potential for noise or blockers to get in the way of your message. Always be aware of what this noise or these blockers could be. The strongest barrier to any message is if it does not address your audience's actual concerns. What is in their mind that could act as a blocker to your message landing in the way you want it to?

It is also important to understand the gap between what you want to say and what people would like to hear. A good internal communications team will listen to the business just as much as they help to shape your messages. It is very easy for your communications to become one-way, top-down messages, simply reflecting the CEO perspective or the official corporate message. It is critical to have an effective way of listening to the team and understanding what they are thinking, what their questions are, and what they are concerned about. Why? Because if you don't address those, the core of your message will never land. Those questions act as barriers in the minds of your people. They will not listen to what you want to say. The cloud generated by their concerns, doubts or questions will block out the key points you want to make. I found this particularly interesting when you travel around the globe.

During a trip to South Africa, I did not know that the team's main concern was about the new local regulation of the Black Economic Empowerment (BEE) programme defined by the government, and what our reaction was going to be.

We had travelled to Johannesburg to launch a new set of products, and we were focused on sharing those new portfolio launches and how the team should sell them. We talked about the potential addressable customer segments and our ambitions in terms of financial results. However, we noticed a lack of real engagement in the room.

Our regional manager took the lead and shared what was really on people's minds. Their concern was that if the company didn't move quickly to address BEE, they would risk losing their jobs, and they may not even be able to do any business there at all, regardless of our new set of products. So they wanted to know, what is the company going to do?

We explained our plans for the region, in line with BEE, and so after addressing that key local question, we could then continue with the rest of our presentation.

My lesson this time was to understand what is on people's minds before trying to connect with them. Of course, your internal communications team and your unit leaders play a key role in identifying the challenges. But it is the leader's role to facilitate the openness to listen to the real concerns of the team.

Deal with cultural diversity

Another relevant stopper that I found critical is cultural diversity. Being aware of the cultural elements of a situation, or the way language is used, will make your communication more successful. There are plenty of stereotypes about every culture, whether you are Spanish, British, German or Chinese. But it is true that culture plays a significant role in communication, whether as a blocker or an enabler. With good awareness, you can create the right level of empathy.

For example, as a Spaniard working in a predominantly British environment, I have observed the importance of the word 'interesting'. Several years ago, I went to the business review of an internet company in Spain. The general manager was presenting the results and their plans. It was not a brilliant one. But his British boss said at the end: "Thank you for the presentation. It has been interesting."

I was shocked – I thought I must have heard a different presentation as I thought it had been poor.

"However," he continued, "the results should have been better, the marketing plan is not clear enough, it needs more detail, and I don't quite believe in the actions you are taking to attract talent."

That day, I learned that 'interesting' is very different from the Spanish 'interesante', and 'interesting' followed by 'however' can be an explosive combination that can demolish any presentation.

I have come across other 'interesting' expressions in a British business environment.

"Maybe you can have another look at your numbers" means "your numbers are rubbish and you need to go and do it all again."

"Maybe we should take this offline" means "if we discuss this here, I will get violent because I disagree so strongly."

While dealing with people from different cultural backgrounds over the years, I learned the importance of understanding those subtle language differences when you communicate.

It is up to you to decide how much you want to immerse yourself culturally when travelling. One of my favourite moments was sharing the end of Ramadan with the head of a local telecommunications company in Dubai. I spent the day meeting our team and I respected the fast for the full day. When sunset came, we went together to Iftar, the important moment when the fast ends. I was pleased to share such an eventful time of the day. He explained to me that fasting for Muslims during Ramadan also includes the increased offering of salat (prayers), recitation of the Quran and doing more good deeds for charity. It was a time to think about those who are less privileged, and act on it. This was a valuable sign of how he was living his religion and why it was important for him. It gave me a unique opportunity to understand better the cultural framework and, in doing so, create connections that can facilitate doing business.

The same happens when you look at how business cards are presented when meeting new people. Many years ago, I met the representatives of a Japanese financial holdings company, and I watched the way they gave the business card carefully with two hands. They expect you to receive the business card in the same way, using two hands and spending a few seconds reading the card. In Japan, handing over a business card represents giving yourself to someone else. To some extent, they replicate themselves in that business card. So, they expect the right level of attention and respect. Taking the card without even looking at it would be considered rude; instead of creating a positive moment, you start off on the wrong foot.

Finally, there is the consideration of big cultural celebrations. Christmas is important to my family and me. But in a truly global organisation, you must show the same respect to Ramadan, Chinese New Year and Diwali, for example. It is also fascinating to learn about these celebrations. Diwali, or Deepvali, the festival of light, celebrates the victory of light over darkness – one of the most important dates in Hinduism. One year, I was in New Delhi at this time and it was a touching experience. When it came to sending my first festive message to the global team that year, I realised that my 'Merry Christmas' expression would not resonate equally everywhere. So I ended my message wishing 'a festive season to everybody and Merry Christmas to those who celebrate it'. It is easy to be inclusive but just as easy to forget the diverse world we live in.

Cultural diversity makes your organisation richer. A team with people from different nationalities can solve a problem better than a group of people who think the same. It is critical to take the time to consider, to understand and reflect on how cultural diversity affects your operations internally and externally.

Listen as much as you talk

The Chief Engagement Officer should be one of the best listeners in the organisation. You must listen systematically and consistently to make sure that the feedback you get is valuable and actionable. It is important to create what I call 'moments of inputs'.

The 'moments of inputs' are those occasions, normally around informal events or meetings, where you are there to receive. You can get suggestions, ideas or questions either around specific areas that concern you or about any topic. One great way we used to do this was through breakfast round tables. 'A breakfast with the CEO' should encourage people to be open, if you create the right climate. Make sure that there are no managers in the room; reinforce the fact that you want to be challenged; listen and ask clarifying questions, but do not judge. I found myself trying to justify why a decision had been made, or why a certain plan was in place, even before letting people finish their point; it took effort to sit and really listen, rather than simply waiting to respond.

That kind of round table discussion can help you understand the concerns of a team in a particular location. It can also shed some light on why some processes might not be working as well as they could. And, of course, it can show you best-in-class practices that should be replicated in other parts of the organisation. Allow people to register of their own accord, but also push for diversity: aim to have the difficult, challenging, disengaged people in the room, not just the supportive ones.

Use the four most powerful words for engagement: What do you think?

CEO agendas are consistently extremely busy, which means that patience is not an easy quality to cultivate. Reviewing projects and making decisions should happen at pace. Very little time is reserved for things that are not action oriented. However, your Engagement dimension needs to kick in here. You should remember to be humble. You must regularly use the four most powerful words for engagement: What do you think? These words can change a conversation. They immediately increase engagement as the person feels you are interested in their point of view and they will feel part of the solution. It will also help you to make sure that every perspective is considered.

We were preparing a presentation for the board and we had a team of graduates helping us. I was debating with my team to decide which key performance indicators would better reflect the progress we had made over the last few quarters. At one point, I turned to ask the three graduates: "What do you think?" They gave us their views and we used them as another input before finishing the slides. A few months later, one of the graduates told me: "I will never forget that moment. The CEO and his team asking for my opinion was a real high that day. It meant that my opinion was important, I was not just producing slides. You changed the confidence I had in myself. Thank you."

I am sure you are, as I am, frequently tempted to give your views very early in any discussion. Next time you have a meeting, try doing the opposite. Ask your colleagues: "What do you think?" and wait until the end to share what you think. I have experimented with this many times in my career. Sometimes you will need to bite your tongue to avoid moving too quickly into 'solution mode'. But the level of engagement you will get is extraordinary, compared to simply telling them what they must do, or even what they should think.

Listen through mentoring

Listening can happen everywhere – in a meeting, in a corridor, or over a coffee. You can also create those personalised moments of listening. Mentoring is a great tool for this. Many believe that mentoring is more about sharing your experience, and telling someone what to do when facing challenges, based on your learning. Fortunately, mentoring can be much more than that. It can create moments where you meet talented people who want to learn how to improve. You should mix mentoring with some good coaching questions to maximise the opportunity. It will encourage you to do three things.

First, you need to articulate the lessons you have learned in ways that you can explain them and make them useful to the people you mentor. It means you must be able to answer difficult questions yourself, like: How do you recommend dealing with a difficult boss? What was the most challenging customer meeting you had? How do you keep learning? In fact, some of those conversations helped me to prepare for some of the content of this book.

Second, you need to understand the context of each individual. This will give you insight into the daily life of your team. What are the issues they face and how do they deal with them? In this sense, it is better if the people you mentor are a diversified team – geographically, by function, gender or ethnicity.

Finally, you need to use the opportunity to ask. People who ask to be mentored are normally willing to make a difference. They have opinions and ways of thinking that may differ from yours. They see things you don't see, they work with parts of the organisation you are not usually exposed to. Be brave and ask for their help. You will be surprised.

Be visible; get out of the ivory tower

A busy agenda with long meetings in your office is your best shield against being exposed to people. Some call it the 'ivory tower'. The temptation of living there, engaging with a selected number of people, thinking that this is what occurs across the world, will end in a distorted sense of reality. It has happened to me. In certain moments, when your agenda is full of 'exciting' internal meetings and discussions on key strategic projects, time becomes a scarce resource. It is easy, then, to receive updates only through channels close to you. My advice is to get a better balance between your internal meetings and your visibility and presence in the organisation.

There is no simpler way to be visible than walking through the office and meeting people. A short chat to discuss what someone is up to, the challenges they are facing, or just how their weekend was, will connect you with them. More importantly, it will provide you with a unique new input, different from all the others you normally get. It is important that wherever you travel to, you create those moments. You will learn about your business and it will help you to 'connect the dots' across geographies, business units and service centres. You can act as a change agent by telling them about what you have seen in other parts of the company. You can become the bee in pollination, using ideas, experiences and tools to make other areas bloom.

Your Engagement dimension will benefit from becoming visible. The empathy, the human touch, the personal close interaction, remain a powerful way to engage. Interacting with people in moments that are not 'pre-organised' will provide you with the opportunity to meet them in their own environment. You can be the 'unexpected CEO' who can take time out of his schedule to meet people. You can choose where you do it (main office vs. a remote office) and how often you do it (having lunch every day in the company canteen vs. visiting one floor every month). It does not matter. Just do it. Talk to people. Ask questions and be prepared to receive them in return.

You can also create visibility systematically as part of a programme, to make sure that the whole leadership team is visible.

We created a programme called 'Back to the Floor'. The idea was to expose senior managers to the actual jobs that people do in distinct areas of the business. We identified roles across the organisation and we chose one day to go 'back to the floor'. That day, 300 managers were paired up with the people doing those jobs.

Our task was to listen and learn about the issues, the help they needed, and shout about the success stories across the business. I went to Brussels to spend the day with the team who were responsible for putting customer orders into the system. We all noticed different things: a significant amount of manual work that could be avoided; lack of definition in some products; and even some physical conditions that needed improvement.

It was a great experience that we repeated a few times and the impact lasted in people's memories. Most of us started our careers in jobs like those. Very quickly we forget what it was like. Always remember where you came from and keep that connection to reality.

Master the art of people recognition

The role of a leader is to provoke and incentivise bottom-up and horizontal communication, just as much as communication from the top. The CEO should be the first to foster informal connections across the organisation.

Sharing news provides a unique opportunity to engage around relevant facts that keep people connected. You might have heard the saying that in any organisation there are people 'who tell the news' and people 'who produce the news'. A good leader can differentiate both. For example, whenever we signed a large customer deal, more often than not, the great success story would be told by someone senior, rather than by the people who signed such a great piece of business. The actual team had been so focused on winning and securing the last final conditions of the contract, they hadn't had time to think about communicating anything. But they were the real heroes, the ones who deserved the recognition.

Make sure you recognise achievements because when this acknowledgement happens, it triggers a lot of benefits. For the individual, it gives them confidence in their personal ability to deliver, and for the rest of the organisation, it identifies a role model, an inspiration for people when it comes to the behaviours the company wants to see more of. In a good working environment, this occurs at all levels: between colleagues, across departments, with customers, top down and bottom up. In my experience, as a highly visible leader you should lead by example. You can create what I call the 'ecosystem of news': a set of connections and relationships between people who enjoy sharing news about the business.

Remember to say thank you

Another area where a small gesture can have a big impact is gratitude. We are not always good at saying thank you or congratulating someone on a job well done, or a great result. This is a powerful message – people like to be thanked, and they enjoy the visibility as an emotional reward.

This motivational recognition can be done spontaneously or in a systematic way. By asking the different units to identify great deliveries, good wins and exceptional efforts on solving issues, you can touch a larger part of your organisation. My recommendation is to spend time defining how you want to use this powerful tool.

I decided to organise a systematic way of recognising individuals and teams who achieved something remarkable. They enjoyed receiving a message directly from the CEO. I was impressed by their responses and, in most cases, I also followed up on those replies.

You are, to some extent, the relationships you create and develop. You don't just share or spread messages, you *are* the message. People will look at you, listen to you and watch your actions. Your visibility as a leader and the shadow you cast can have a big influence on how the rest of the organisation operates. Consider the saying: 'What you are doing speaks so loudly that I can't hear what you are saying'. How you behave every day will determine your ability to influence in the organisation. The atmosphere you create will help your business objectives and it will become part of the leadership style of the organisation.

Recognise the invisible people

Think about those people who are less visible to you. You see them and maybe you even say hello to them. But do you know anything about them? Have you ever had the feeling that you are transparent and that you don't exist for the people around you? This is often how people feel in the presence of senior leaders. Smiling, and saying good morning or good evening, matters to them – whether they are the person on reception, your office cleaner, or a colleague just a few levels down. Just a few words of recognising their existence can make a huge difference to them and the rest of their team. We all contribute. It is easy to forget but worth remembering.

In all this communication activity, the Chief Engagement Officer has to keep three key attributes: being open, honest and personal, to deliver the maximum potential when connecting and building empathy with every stakeholder. Some people think that it is better to have an opaque relationship with your people. I believe that for the wider team it is really valuable to know the person behind the job. You are yourself first and your job second. You don't need to be everybody's friend. But you have to keep the openness when you communicate, when you speak with people and when you get feedback.

Openness is being prepared to explain why things happen, especially under difficult circumstances. And honesty is being able to admit when you have made a mistake, and you need to make a special effort to fix it. Sharing successes, challenges and reality will build the credibility that is the very basis for bringing the organisation along with you on the journey. Finally, engagement is personal. A CEO job is impossible without making it personal. You have to be 'all in' and it should be apparent in your communications.

Communicate with all stakeholders

For the CEO, engagement should be your way of keeping as many stakeholders as possible connected to the vision of the company, to make sure they support it. This is where your Evangelist dimension should work together with the Engagement dimension. In addition to the team, there are other key stakeholder groups to spend time with, to gain their backing: customers, the board, the press, analyst and investor communities, and society, including political and regulatory bodies.

It is essential to engage customers in your vision. They should realise that they are at the core of the ambition of the company. It will encourage them to buy your products and services. They will be part of your growth and continuous improvement.

The board should discuss, understand and feel part of the vision, and how it creates value. They are representing shareholders and they aim to guarantee the right governance. Board members individually can help in regional strategies, they can act as soundboards for portfolio developments, and they can even participate in events internally or with customers. Involving the board will facilitate the implementation of the vision.

The external market must also engage at different levels. The press provides a great channel to the greater market, and positive coverage will help. It means paying attention and learning the different ways of working in diverse publications. Help them to provide news, and they will be more interested in your organisation.

You should spend a significant amount of time engaging analysts and investors. They can help to focus the business and make it better. Their questions and challenges will make you think and reflect on the vision. In some moments of the lifecycle of a company, the investor community could require a lot of your focus as CEO. This is where a good combination of the three dimensions can gain their confidence and build credibility with them. You will need the three basic components: a clear vision, a good connection and a solid performance.

In heavily regulated industries, dealing well with regulatory bodies and political authorities will be crucial. A good shared understanding of their priorities and your business imperatives will help. Being strong and clear on your principles doesn't mean a bad relationship. Robust conversations are necessary, and the CEO's leadership should be visible to represent the company's best interests.

Finally, you will need to engage people from other society bodies, such as non-governmental organisations (NGOs), universities, or local governments. You must decide how you and your team spend your time. The stronger the engagement of your organisation with all stakeholders, the easier it will be to accomplish the vision you have defined. However, you should agree who in your management team is doing what, and when.

We were hosting an event for European journalists in our research centre. Visiting the labs is an opportunity to understand future development. You always discover new ideas that are being tested, technologies being stressed and partnerships that can create new solutions. It was a great opportunity for the journalists to ask about technologies they were aiming to know more about.

The organiser wanted to use the opportunity for the journalists to get to know us better, to understand what they were interested in, and even to create a network amongst them. We knew it would help to make them more open to listening to news during the year if we were more open to them. At the same time, if they have doubts or challenges, it is better to receive those questions directly in a lively session, instead of reading them for the first time in an article.

So, I decided to make sure they knew how important they were to us. As the organiser started the introductions, I memorised their face, name and area of interest. I remember them even now – Geert, Paul, Ana, Pilar… and so on. It was tricky but I was determined not to fail. We had 16 journalists from 10 countries, with very different areas of interest, from connected cars to high-speed broadband using G.Fast technologies.

When we moved to the dining table, I gave the welcome speech and I managed to mention each of them and their topic of interest. The surprise was written all over their faces. They appreciated the effort. Somehow, it was a way of showing that they mattered to us. It was a small gesture that had a great engagement impact and facilitated conversations, interviews and articles in the following months.

Engage through the power of being positive

The Chief Evangelist Officer's passion and the Chief Engagement Officer's positive attitude will help when it comes to executing plans. There is a fine line between being optimistic and being out of touch with reality. I am a positive person and my optimism has helped me through difficult times. During difficult times, your team will look to you for guidance, listening not only to your words but also to the tone you use. There is always a balance to be found between optimism and realism.

As the saying goes: 'The pessimist complains about the wind; the optimist expects it to change; the positive realist adjusts the sails.' The CEO's influence can determine the attitude of the team. Being positive means developing a can-do attitude, identifying the negative spots and making the team believe to perform.

To move people into 'making things happen' territory, they should be thinking positively. It is common to find people discussing the reasons why a project or a task can't be done, or why a specific target will not be achieved. The CEO, like any other leader, can change the attitude quite easily. Instead of asking why something won't happen, ask: "What do we need to do to make it happen?"

We were discussing how to launch a new tariff that could disrupt the market and help our position in the high bandwidth services business. A product manager came to the meeting and started his presentation explaining all the reasons why it was not possible to launch the product when we wanted to do it. His arguments were solid: we didn't have proper systems, the platforms weren't yet proven enough, it was difficult to find the right expertise in the market, and we had challenges in training salespeople. We changed the tone of the meeting by taking a different approach: "Let us start discussing what we have to do to overcome the issues to launch it, instead of admiring the problem and listing the reasons why we can't do it."

We ended up with a clear plan, with timelines for the system changes, a training plan and investment approvals. We rescheduled the launch date to a more realistic one, and we converted a negative discussion into a positive one with just a small but profound change: moving into a can-do attitude.

This inspirational approach can help address 'impossible' tasks. I feel inspired by so many examples of achievements that looked impossible when facing them.

This is how I felt when I met the BT Sport team. We had an inspiring introduction from the COO of BT Sport, who personified what it means to make the impossible possible. He explained how they built the studio and prepared to launch within just a few months, while previous projects took several years to build. I particularly enjoyed his description of the moment they were told that it was not possible to use the intended building, due to a number of very well justified reasons. He went through each one, asking why and providing a solution or an alternative and, by the end, the conclusion was that it was feasible to set up the studio there. I wondered how many times we accept a 'no' instead of getting deeper into the 'why not' and addressing those actions to make it happen.

Reflection

In this chapter, we discussed how to develop your Engagement dimension to connect with your team and other key stakeholders. Consider the following questions:

- How much time do you spend preparing your messages and deciding which channels to use to deliver them?

- Which channels do you use to communicate, both formally and informally?

- What are the main blockers you have found in communication? How do you deal with them?

- How do you make personal connections with your team or your colleagues? How much do you know about their lives? What motivates them?

- How often do you recognise others in front of their bosses? How do you say thank you?

- What types of cultural diversity challenges have you faced? What mistakes will you never repeat again?

CHAPTER V

LEVERAGE THE POWER OF THE TEAM

The Chief Engagement Officer is the most important custodian of the quality of the team implementing the vision. He must be a role model when it comes to making sure people become one of the strongest assets of the organisation. It means actively selecting, developing, organising, coaching and empowering the team. You can have a great technical product, a solid customer base and an exceptional financial performance, but to make it sustainable, you need a strong team who can take care of it and move it to the next level of excellence. Team, for me, includes all levels of the organisation, but it starts with the group of people who work directly for you. Be bold and don't make trade-offs on recruiting, changing and developing your core team.

Select the team

Selecting your direct team is one of the most urgent and important tasks for a CEO. In most cases, you will inherit a group of people assigned to specific roles. Regardless of how good they are, it does not mean they are the right people to implement the vision. A new appointment is a unique opportunity to confirm or change each of the members of your direct team. Most CEOs regret not being quick enough to make those decisions. There are two questions that you must be able to answer as soon as possible. First: Who is in? Who is passionately backing the vision without any doubt, and is prepared to face the challenges that will appear? Second: Who has the capabilities, skills or the potential for the actions that are required?

The question "Are you in?" does not need to be as dramatic as Sir Ernest Shackleton's advert to recruit people for his Nimrod Antarctic expedition in 1907. But it should still inspire people and reflect the need to be prepared to run a risk when starting a significant project or transformation journey. Whenever I have used it, it always brings the spirit of adventure to the moment.

> **Men wanted** for hazardous journey. Low wages, bitter cold, long hours of complete darkness. Safe return doubtful. Honour and recognition in event of success.

It reflects what I found in every relevant project I have ever been involved in. It is a journey, sometimes a hard one, with dark moments that require resilience. The ambition is to get through it. The main reward is personal pride and, in some cases, recognition.

When looking at the capabilities and skills of your team, you need to balance their current roles with the ability to learn and take on other jobs. Whether you have been hired from outside of the organisation, or promoted from the existing team, getting your team right and early is probably the most important ingredient for success.

When you inherit a team, in reality it is a set of individuals with jobs, responsibilities and their own history. The initial analysis is to check whether they have the capabilities, the attitude and the potential required for the tasks that they would tackle as an individual and as a team. As part of your planning, it is key to assess those three elements, so make sure you conduct personal interviews to figure out the situation of each member of the team.

Selecting the team is a complicated task because you aren't just choosing the team for today. You are choosing a group that will navigate the changes to come, whether they are due to the market, the vision, or the business imperatives. Different phases of transformation may require singular capabilities. The skills required for an expansion plan are very different from those required for a large restructuring. The kind of individuals you will need may change and your team must be prepared to adapt to new circumstances.

Good to Great by James Collins is one of my favourite books on leadership. He discusses what makes a company become a great one, instead of just being a good one. "Good is the enemy of great," he says. I think it is true. Good is not enough. It requires strong discipline on the vision, the execution, and the people.

The recipe for greatness is based on a strong leader with core attributes including vision, determination and humility. The next component is the team; he refers to getting on the bus, and then making sure the destination is defined. This is why, several times in my career, I have asked members of the team: "Are you in? Are you part of the team? Are you committed to others, and to what we are going to face together?" They must be explicit about their commitment to you and the rest of the team, acknowledging it openly and loudly, and backing it up with facts.

An interesting situation is when you have been promoted above your peers. In my career, I have experienced it: I have been asked to lead the team I was previously a member of. It is not an easy situation as you have different relationships with them. You also take on a different perspective when you become the boss, and you can demand more from those you feel were not delivering as much as they should. You will also need to create the alliances with those who are ready to work with you. You may find that some of them might not want to be part of the team. You can give them another chance if you are clear on what you expect. But in some cases, you will need to accept that a friend should go. Be prepared for it. Honesty and clarity will help in such challenging moments.

Identify your 'extended' team

When it comes to selecting the team, you will also need to define who is in your core team, and who belongs to what I call 'the extended team'. You can look at it as though you have three levels.

The first is a small group of three or four people who will help you to make decisions quickly, drive execution fast and test ideas rapidly. In my case, this group was made up of the Chief Finance Officer, the HR Director and the Strategy Director.

The second group includes the rest of your direct reports. They run the business and make things happen. However, in my experience, it is not only the direct reports who constitute the team that will implement the vision and lead the transformation you aim to make in your organisation. So the third group consists of the people who report to the executive leadership team, and these are the people you need to create a direct, two-way connection with – of course, with the support and acceptance of your direct team. On one hand, you will create a more agile organisation if you can deliver messages directly to them and get their commitment. But you will also gain a richer set of feedback, ideas and challenges from them and they are the ones who can tell you the truth about what is happening in the field.

Once, I sent a personalised email to each of the 120 senior managers about what we should do differently. To tailor each one to their area of expertise took me a lot of time. I asked specific questions, but also encouraged them to come back with other topics they thought we were missing or overlooking. I learned a lot from those email exchanges. Some triggered further meetings, or made us reconsider our plans.

Of course, you must be ready to hear things that are not nice. They could challenge the way the strategy or plans are being executed. You should listen and respond, engage in a conversation about what could be done differently, identify the actions to tackle and areas to improve. Be as specific as possible. Never accept a generic 'service is bad' statement. Ask for details and be ready to discuss them, to find out the facts but avoid being protective or defensive. The risk of missing such an opportunity is also a ticket for failure in the future. If you take the action to ask, you must close the loop with each of them personally. You are not doing it because it is a nice 'marketing' action. You are doing it because you really value what they think, what they experience every day in front of the customer.

Some of the responses you would get will be long, with a lot of detail; others will just ask questions about our plans, and ask why we are doing certain things that require a lot of work but produce no value in the field. This is what I learned. Cultivating a larger, well-engaged team is time consuming, but it is worth keeping the connection and a lively interaction. They are your team.

Develop the team

A team is also a dynamic entity. It changes, evolves and transforms over time, affected by internal and external factors. Each member is also subject to a personal journey. So, you must look at how each member develops and you should drive this development. In order to do this, you must understand the strengths of each person, their potential succession plans, and how you can enrich the team over time, where diversity and fresh talent play a key role.

By understanding their strengths, you will make better decisions. More analytical profiles will be invaluable when it comes to financial planning. More empathetic characters will add value to challenging customer conversations. It is not just about the job they do, it is about their contribution. A great test of the team's development is to consider which players could have a different position by the end of their development plan. The plan can be as formal as you decide but, in any case, it should be part of your personal conversations with each of them.

I remember several discussions about career development, knowledge and skills with my team. In one discussion, for example, our Chief Information Officer shared his aspiration to run a business in the future. So, in addition to his existing responsibilities, we assigned him a small unit where he could expand his knowledge and see what it was like to run a business unit with profit and loss (P&L) responsibility. After a year and half, he was ready to run one of the larger business units. We took advantage of his deep technology expertise and his strength in executing projects, and spent time helping him to improve his customer engagement and financial knowledge. As a result, not only had he developed as an individual but also we had a stronger team.

To have this flexibility in rotating people, you need to prepare proper succession plans. It means thinking well in advance about who could be ready to take a new role, either immediately or within a few months or years. It also means you need to be exposed to as many people as possible – in presentations, meeting and projects. The best way to assess someone is through his actual performance in a job. It can be complemented with some external advice from specialised companies. A strong plan like this will allow you to rotate people and jobs, and you can also use it to put people outside of their comfort zone if you want to have more rounded leaders. Some global companies, for example, demand country management experience before you are eligible for a top executive position, because they consider that kind of exposure to a domestic business to be critical.

These succession plans pass their test when the CEO leaves. If someone on the successors list replaces him, it is a sign of good preparation and internal talent development.

My successor and I worked together for nine years. I hired him to run a regional operation and he had several responsibilities in different regions. He was ready, which meant that we could make a smooth transition. His deep knowledge of customers, the business and the team helped him to enter the role quickly and effectively. This meant the organisation could keep up the momentum, avoiding a stop-start effect. Of course, he would execute with his own style, and he would make changes to the strategy and the way the business is run – each CEO aims to leave his own stamp on the organisation. But again, this is why he was ready.

Benefit from the value of a diverse team

When you build and develop your direct team and your organisation, you are also responsible for fostering the diversification of talent, and diversity of any kind must be taken seriously. You must be able to embrace talent from as many sources as possible, to guarantee the longevity and future success of your business. You must also be able to attract diverse talent to your organisation. This is not a tick box exercise to enforce fairness; it will enrich your organisation. At the same time, your attitude towards and understanding of diversity will make you a more successful leader.

This also applies to your direct team. As a CEO, it is very easy to feel more comfortable with people that think like you do, who have had a similar education to you, who work in similar ways or even have similar experience. It is great to share common backgrounds in some areas, but the more diverse you make your team, the stronger it will be. And this is not only about gender, ethnicity or sexual orientation; I am also referring to thought leadership. It is difficult sometimes to accept someone in the team who is bringing a new angle, or questioning why a decision has been taken. But this is what makes a better team. Having people around you who can tell you the truth, challenge your ideas and come with new proposals is essential. Your role is to foster diversity, and the foundation for this is to have a team with diverse individuals.

One way of getting actively involved is through specific programmes which promote diversity in the organisation. You can help others to reflect and discuss it openly. Diversity should be a proactive question every leader should make. It does not mean making the wrong but politically correct decision when appointing the best candidate for a job, it is the opposite: appointing the person who will make it a more diverse, therefore stronger, team.

For example, we took part in a programme called the 30% Club, which intended to enable that discussion. I thought the topic was so relevant that I decided to write a blog about it.

Do you embrace diversity?

Embracing diversity is becoming more and more a key strategic opportunity for companies and organisations. The richness of having a diverse set of team members gives a wider perspective, a way to innovate in the way you look at problems or consider business alternatives. There are several ways of looking at diversity and one of the most relevant is gender diversity.

We held a mentoring sponsor event with the 30% Club and Women Ahead, and I had the privilege of hosting the event. The 30% Club aims to get to a minimum of 30% women into FTSE-100 executive and board positions. In 2016, the figure stands at 26.1%, up from 12.5% in 2010 when the Club launched.

We are participating in the 30% Club's cross-company mentoring scheme, which aims to develop the pipeline and parity of women on boards. Mentees are all high-potential women, from a variety of levels. I am proud that we have eight people being mentored by executives of other participating companies.

Many times we forget to reflect how we can ensure we value diversity in all our decision processes. Lots of studies show that diversified organisations deliver stronger performance. Diversity gives us the opportunity to be a better company, a better team.

Gender diversity, like the one fostered by the programme above, is key. It requires attention, from the recruitment process to the way promotions are done, from the way jobs are offered to the way we define the access route to senior positions. In many organisations, there are active programmes to promote this gender diversity. But not everybody believes it is good to implement these proactive policies and focus. I am convinced it is still necessary. I feel fortunate to know a good number of excellent female professionals and leaders, starting with my wife who has developed a brilliant career. They have done it while raising families and having strong family commitments. We should appreciate the additional effort that, in most cases, they had to put in to get where they are.

As a leader, the question is how to encourage and facilitate the opportunities for diverse groups of people to enrich the team you are creating. In business, what you don't measure is unlikely to improve. So, a key element of these pro-diversity policies is the KPIs you define around them. For example, we tracked the diversity of people in the recruitment process and the diversity of those we finally recruited; we tracked the diversity of those who moved to the next level of the organisation, and the salaries for similar jobs in different diversity groups. It is key that you personally take the time to talk to both successful individuals and to those who have been rejected. You can also nominate a 'diversity champion' to provide more visibility to this key topic. However, the CEO must be the strongest champion as well. This, of course, also applies to other types of diversity such as ethnicity or sexual orientation, which require similar attention – not only to avoid discrimination but also to encourage integration, which enriches the organisation.

Acquire talent

The Chief Engagement Officer should also be the main sponsor of talent programmes. He must provoke the rest of the organisation, forcing it to create space for new talent to contribute, grow and transform the organisation they work in. Talent should be attracted, developed, and discarded when it doesn't fit. Of course, it is true that everybody has talent. But I am referring here to situations where a particular area needs a fresh focus. You can bring talent on board to refresh your way of thinking, bring people from a new generation or from a different background. I learned that it is healthy to identify streams of talent to be dropped into specific areas of the company and help them to navigate freely later.

My four kids are in their twenties, at the start of their careers. This is probably another reason why I am so sure that the blend of solid, experienced, talented people with fresh joiners is a powerful mix. I see what young people can bring. Graduate and apprentice programmes provide the opportunity to incorporate new talent with different perspectives from your own. The curiosity, energy and open-mindedness are invaluable assets to mix with the knowledge, passion for customers and experience that your organisation could already have. You have to seize the opportunity to allow everything you do to be challenged, processes to be questioned and new solutions to be considered. I know that the so-called millennials could scare organisations off. They challenge the status quo, and you need to keep an open mind in order to listen, and be prepared to move and change.

As an example, I enjoyed meeting 25 new apprentices, the latest recruits to the BT Security team. I told them that in many ways they were the new 'Kingsman' team that we needed, to face the growing challenges in the cybersecurity space that appear every day. Their fast learning curve means we could develop qualified experts who serve customers in an area of growth.

I also spent time with a group of 30 new graduates, sharing my personal experience when I started in a similar role many years ago in IBM. They asked clever questions about the business, and they also wanted to know about the path to becoming a CEO. No fear, no taboo, just curiosity. I loved being challenged and interacting with the fresh talent joining the company. But it is also your responsibility to retain them, giving them challenges to confront.

These kind of programmes also provide you with the chance to embrace diverse talent. One of the best encounters I experienced was with a graduate called Will. His challenges, and how he was facing them, were a source of inspiration for me. It reminded me that we are responsible for making sure that nothing gets in the way of acquiring talent. Will was deaf but that did not stop him from working hard and learning throughout his graduate rotations. I was impressed by the way he communicated using a tablet. When I was speaking to him, on the phone, someone on the line was typing and he was able to read what I was saying. He admitted to being really good at lip-reading, and he was even able to recognise different accents like mine.

I considered how important it is to make it easier for people with challenges to integrate so that they can share their strengths fully. Will was just another reason to feel inspired about how the power of communications can change the lives of people, making a better world.

Develop talent

After acquiring talent, you must also develop it. However, that is not the role of Human Resources, as it is frequently assumed. Business leaders, starting with the CEO, should act as the owners of any talent programme. The power and value of today's cohort can transform today's business, but even more importantly, they will be the foundation of tomorrow. We live in a world in which new generations are interacting and using technology in different ways, buying goods and services using different channels, and reassessing their priorities for their life and what they expect at work. They are also more demanding when it comes to a company's social contribution, creating an open environment of sharing information and ideas, and evolving careers within a company.

We decided to create some cohorts of people with the ambition and potential to become the next leaders in the business. We wanted to create a community across boundaries, so we brought together 10 groups of people from different regions and units. The teams took away key business problems and worked together to put forward ideas or proposals to fix them. We called it the Future Leaders programme. I hosted the meetings and we discussed two things. First, the areas they felt we should be acting on, to develop further or to change. Second, I had a number of areas I wanted them to work on.

For example, they looked at how we manage global accounts, and how we could improve the way we resource critical projects. They acted like a think tank. We shared the outcomes with the operational owners. It motivated the future leaders as they felt excited about the opportunity to contribute beyond their day jobs. For the leadership team, it was the chance to have more exposure to the talent of the organisation, and to help them to improve through the process.

Organise the team

Leading a team is one of the most fascinating experiences anyone can have, and the more senior they are, the more difficult it is. They are individuals with a lot of experience, different motivations and distinct capabilities. Learning how to combine those skills, and to get the best out of them, requires time. You must know each of them well – their past, their personal core, and what they are aiming for. Why are they in this project? Collecting the individual answers will help you to create the best way of working and, consequently, make it a stronger team.

One person came from a poor family, and so he was over-demanding of himself and the people who worked with him. One person had made money when he sold his company years ago, but still wanted to feel the pride of achieving great things. For most of them, making an impact and being able to leave a legacy behind was a strong focus, and they all loved to work with customers, willing to provide a high-level service. But they had doubts about themselves and their teams, they questioned part of our way of working, the way we were organised, and the fact that responsibility was not as clearly allocated as it should be. Bureaucracy and heavy processes produced frustration, and we needed to work together to remove it. They all wanted to do the right things, to succeed personally and to be part of a winning team. So, they were ready to do their best to make a difference.

Once you understand your team, it is time to decide how you will run it to make the most of the individuals. When you lead a global organisation, you must make one key decision: Do I manage them as a team or as a group of individuals with interdependencies? I found it brilliantly explained in the book *Speed Lead* by Kevan Hall.

You can always find specific projects that bring the whole team around a common goal that requires joint execution. In a global organisation, for example, you work together to define the strategy, the direction of travel. Someone should bring the framework of that strategy, to generate the debate and to reach an agreed or supported position. But regardless of these common goals, it is very difficult to force diverse leaders to work together if there is no clear benefit for them in doing so.

When I joined, we had organised our customer-facing units around two categories: geography and industry. There were continuous discussions about where the limits of accountability lay. Of course, customers were managed from one single division. But there were smaller decisions, like travelling approvals, which made things difficult in our day-to-day jobs. We decided to change and split the business into four geographical units, whilst still providing unified service to global customers. It meant that there was a primary focus on delivering against the regional targets, and you can mitigate the silo effect by sharing some key targets. But you should avoid diluting accountability by trying to foster collaboration. Collaboration must be an integral part of the skill set and behaviours of your leadership team. They must foster a team spirit, ready to support others and drive their success as well as their own. But this is not always the case, and the way you lead to embrace that way of working is critical.

I met a senior vice president of an industry analyst firm. He described the transformation his company was going through. The nature of their business previously was to work with a degree of independence. However, the trends of the industry and the requirements from customers started to demand a more cohesive way of working. Their analysts needed to work as a team to leverage the value of their knowledge. They had to change the way they worked, without losing the value of those 'gurus' and their expertise on the subjects they had mastered. He compared it to a rock band; they could no longer afford to have solo players working alone, no more groups of isolated artists. He said that they had to play like a rock band. A global one. I still remember his story and I have used it several times. Each member of the band is a subject matter expert in his instrument, but they have to play in sync to deliver great performance. Only then will they be greater than the sum of their parts.

In such a scenario, you must act as a facilitator, understanding each member of your team, and creating the atmosphere to make the magic of teamwork happen. To do it, you must set clear responsibilities for each person and set the ambition for the team. The organisation is like one large system that works through subsystems. If you aim to optimise individual subsystems separately, you will underperform.

In one of our management meetings, we used the example of a football team. If you consider the football team as the system, the optimal desired outcome would be winning the match. However, if you allow each subsystem of players (goalkeeper, defenders, midfielders and forwards) to aim for the best results they can get, they will not win.

The forwards alone would be happy to score as many goals as possible – to them, four would be better than one. But as a team, it would be a better outcome to win 1-0, only scoring one goal but winning, than losing 4-5. Getting the team to work together on a common goal is an art. The way you have structured your organisation is just the means to an end. The structure will never be the objective, and you should be ready to change it if it is not serving its purpose.

In this sense, the design of an organisation can make a difference to its performance. For instance, most companies use a matrix model to run their operations. A matrix model means that any given function of the company will have two reporting lines.

We once had a regional Finance Director working for the Regional President but reporting directly to the Chief Finance Officer of the group. One of my colleagues in Singapore needed to gain approval for a business trip. The decision needed two approvers to sign it off, adding a degree of unnecessary tension and reducing the agility to make a decision. In this kind of situation, you need clarity on accountability and trust. You can allocate accountability but you need to encourage trust. So, we changed the way budgets were managed and allowed the decision to be taken locally.

Some people struggle with a matrix organisation. But there is a rationale to it because, on one hand, being closer to the field will help you make informed decisions. At the same time, you need consistency across the enterprise, for example, on policies of cash management. It is important for both bosses to provide the right level of support, instead of stressing out the individual. An easy way that worked for us in a good number of cases was to have the strategy, policies and plans defined by the central functions, and local units being responsible for adapting and executing them – all working under the principle of having aligned targets.

Coach the team

The CEO must be the 'super coach' of the organisation, starting with his team but not limited to it. In coaching, he can help people to find what motivates them, define joint ambitions, and have tough conversations when needed.

Different people have different views of winning. For sales-oriented groups, it is about signing a deal with a customer. For others, it is about completing a technology project. In all cases, it is about achieving. Therefore, the questioning in a coaching conversation can help to find those inner objectives and ambitions that will get the best out of everyone.

Your knowledge and experience will make you a great coach. Your direct team will appreciate if you have humble, not patronising, conversations and discuss openly the challenges they face. Steering the direction of each one within the team will help the group.

We were having discussions about why the service was not as good as we wanted and, in some cases, it was because we were selling too many bespoke (non-standard) solutions. There was a robust debate between the heads of the different units with this responsibility. Initially, they began pointing fingers, keen to shift the blame. We hosted a session with them and, just using questions about the pain points and concerns, we identified the roots of the problem. The first and most important issue was to make people in every deal work together when making the offer to the customer. We were the main problem by not pushing for proposals to be built jointly. It is easy too for sales to say that service is bad, or for service to say that sales teams sell projects that are impossible to deliver. But it is also useless. Coaching a team to work differently will make a difference.

Coaching conversations can happen at any moment, and about any kind of topic. They can also inspire and challenge the team to do things they considered impossible. I often found myself jumping into solution mode, finding the final answer instead of taking the team through the reflection. It is much more effective to be patient. One technique is to keep asking the question "Why?" until you get to the root cause. We all know it and it pays off.

Many years ago, we wanted to put our logo on top of our office building in Madrid, in a highly noticeable place. It was a nice way of making our brand more visible. When we asked why it was not there already, we were told that the owner of the building would not allow it. Why? Because we were not the only company in the building, and the other companies may want their logos up there too. It could create a dispute for the best place to put the logo. So we offered to take the second best place. But it was still impossible. Why? It would cost a huge amount. Why? When we called the landlord, he said it was just to discourage us from asking again. So, we agreed a new price and the location of the logo, keeping options for others in the future. A few weeks later, our logo was there, on top of the roof of one of the tallest and most visible places in Madrid. Just by asking "Why?"

Be ready to have tough conversations

Tough conversations are part of the CEO role. Engagement is not only about positive, rewarding messages. You must be prepared for the difficult moments. Whether it is about poor business performance, a personal issue, or a discussion about leaving the company. I learned that clarity, honesty and decisiveness are all important.

Be clear: those conversations should be based in facts. A tough discussion should never get emotional from your side. Regardless of how you feel, you must remain objective and very specific. It will facilitate the challenging moment.

Be honest and open. We are all adults, and the worst thing is to make the situation worse by hiding behind other decision makers, or even lying. Take your time, and do it in a proper environment. You should not have a difficult conversation in a rush, where you don't have the time to listen, and these discussions deserve privacy.

Be decisive: the sooner you execute, the better. Once you have decided to have the conversation, have it. Time just deteriorates the situation. Define a time frame for executing whatever outcome you expect. If it is about improving a situation, define a clear plan and when it is going to be reviewed. If you are asking someone to leave the company, be bold when it comes to when and how.

One of the most difficult moments is when you must have this exit conversation with someone who is not just a colleague but also a friend. A few years ago, I had one of these conversations. I appreciated the person a lot; we had worked together for several years, he was good in some of his functions and proactive in a few areas. But it was time to make a change. We had tried for some time to transform the unit he was leading and the results were not coming through. I was open about it: you have not achieved what we agreed, so we should move on before it gets worse. Of course, it was not easy for either of us. I prepared it well, thinking carefully about the message and the person. I learned to separate the respect and appreciation I felt for the person from the facts. We will all have conversations like this one day, so treat everybody as you would like to be treated when the time comes.

Empower the team

The Chief Engagement Officer should leverage the power of the whole organisation, which means you need to free everyone's individual energy. This is, for me, the sense of empowering: it means people can operate at their maximum potential. Empowerment can become a way of fostering imagination, innovation and speed. With a more empowered organisation, decisions can be made faster, and closer to the front of the business. But you must be clear on the objectives, processes and governance to make sure that empowerment does not generate unknown risks. You need clarity on the boundaries, flexibility to allow failure, but also putting proper consequence management in place.

Empowerment always exists within a framework of operation. Flexibility and agility in decision making must happen within these agreed boundaries – such as establishing a limit of discounts that can be provided to customers, or the priorities in the delivery of a project. When someone is asking to be more empowered, I find they actually have more power than they think. Normally, those who do not ask are already able to handle the organisation better and pull the levers available.

One common misunderstanding about empowerment is around the definition of that framework or context. You must clarify the degrees of freedom and where they apply. Empowerment is not the right to do whatever you want. It is the ability to operate flexibly within the limits of a defined model.

In a discussion about empowerment with one of our teams, I used the following story.

In a classical orchestra, roles and musical instruments are clearly allocated. If you play the violin, you know your role. The most beautiful concerts are delivered when the conductor manages to leverage the skills of the musicians during the time they are playing. Would you say that orchestra members are empowered? Imagine that they are playing *Carmen* by Bizet. Empowerment does not mean that a violinist can bring the sheets of Verdi's *Aida*. There is a framework within which everybody should be playing. The wrong empowerment could be bringing a guitar, instead of a violin, to the rehearsals. The role of the violinist is to play the violin part in *Carmen*. That is the framework of operations. He is empowered to decide how to play, keeping the instrument fit, and putting all of his personal energy into every note, delivering the best possible performance.

The feeling of empowerment also liberates your energy to do your absolute best within the framework in which you operate. Having disempowered people would be less effective and less engaging, delivering worse results and being unhappy. If you give people the confidence and freedom to make proposals, discuss openly and make their own mistakes, they will be happier to make or propose decisions. You will enter a virtuous circle because they will keep making better and more agile choices.

We were at the Liverpool International Business Festival. The marketing team was thrilled to be a part of it. At the end of one day, we met with a few graduates who worked in the marketing department. After some time chatting about the event, their role and how they saw what we were doing in Liverpool, I took the opportunity to ask what they thought we should do better or differently in our business. Silence. They looked at each other. They were probably thinking: Do we run the risk of telling the CEO our honest opinion?

One of them took the risk. "Luis, we believe there is lack of empowerment in the field. We are always waiting for decisions from the top. Even if we are convinced that something does not make sense, we cannot just do it." I asked them for an example.

"We organise monthly dinners with a few customers. We believe it is a waste of time and money. Even those who attend only do it because they feel obliged to. But we keep doing them, and spending time and effort to organise them. We don't see the value, for us or for our customers."

I asked if they had made a proposal about their views. They had not, so I suggested they put together their proposal, and when I discussed it with the head of marketing, we toasted the graduates and their boldness. A few days later, I received an email from the most vocal of the graduates. They prepared the proposal the following day and, in the same week, the marketing team agreed to stop these events. She said: "We realised that empowerment may not be just a top-down thing. Thanks for challenging us."

Make clear that empowerment comes with accountability

Empowerment is also a contract with each of your employees. With empowerment comes accountability. You will have to accept that they will do things differently from you, they may take actions more slowly because of their learning curve, and they may well make mistakes. This is all part of creating a more empowered organisation. I would have never learned anything if my bosses had always told me what to do, how to do it, and when.

An easy way to encourage people at the beginning is by asking the question: "What would you do?" You can ask this when facing any decision. This also applies when people come to you with a problem, aiming to delegate the resolution to you. The best way is to make them think and come back with proposals. You should also ask them to choose their top proposal. It will force them to contemplate different scenarios and evaluate which one is the one they would select. Then you can discuss and offer your viewpoint. If you give them your answer in the first instance, you are encouraging the wrong behaviour and they will keep coming to you for decisions.

Having the right processes to help people make decisions can also foster empowerment. This will give clarity on the responsibilities, and it will encourage them to be proactive where they can influence. It will help people to keep focus and avoid wasting time and energy.

We were preparing our budgets for the following year. One key area is where you invest money to maintain or grow your business, where capital expenditure (capex) is spent. In a meeting to discuss how that capex was allocated, the topic of empowerment came to the table.

The Finance Director was quite clear: "We don't have an unlimited capex budget; every project competes with others, and they must demonstrate their returns to get the approval. We, as the investment committee, have the responsibility to set the rules and define the priorities and approve where we will invest."

Someone said that it could disengage people as they expected more power, more decision-making capability.

The Finance Director continued: "They are totally empowered to decide which investment they want to pursue and present them here. They have the empowerment to build their business cases and involve all the units they need, and they will bring it to the committee and decide how to defend it. It is in their hands to make a great case, to prepare it well, show the returns and define a solid rollout proposal. Once they get the approval, their empowerment brings the responsibility of executing and delivering. Those who want more power just need to be more proactive, building better investment cases and being prepared to take the risk of deciding and executing."

Apply consequence management

Two apparently contradicting forces should support empowerment: applying consequence management whilst allowing failure as a source of learning.

Consequence management is all about recognising successes and failures, and understanding the root causes of both. A positive recognition of a great outcome will reinforce the same attitude and approach in other situations. By making it visible, the rest of the team will be ready to take similar risks. But when failure happens, there must be consequences too. If the decision or the execution ended in a bad result, it is important to learn why. People should also understand that the organisation will not tolerate certain situations. If the root causes are due to a lack of attention, wrong behaviour or deliberately not following the right governance, you should act.

Many years ago, we found a team that was systematically installing equipment without doing the right final testing. Of course, they had all the empowerment to do it right, they could decide when and how to do it, but they were not. We changed not only the team in the field but also their manager, because he had allowed it to happen. He had not created a spirit to do the right things. I learned that while you should always provide freedom and flexibility, you also should be ready to manage the consequences in a fair but determined way.

However, making mistakes is also inevitable, as not all decisions will be the right ones. By quickly identifying which ones were wrong, why, and taking an action to resolve them, the whole organisation will learn. It is the same with your kids as they are growing up. It is insane to try to control them and make all the decisions for them. Your role as a parent is to support them, provide advice if they ask, and let it go to allow them to grow.

I was tempted several times to intervene and decide, instead of being silent and letting the team decide and execute what they thought was right – even if it was a small decision. I remember being asked about which kind of furniture to put in a new floor. Of course, I had an opinion, but if you give it, you will end up being asked about every single detail – which will take up your time and attention. On the other hand, when asked about some customer strategies, I always told the team that they had a better view than me. I could give an opinion, but to have a stronger workforce, you must let it go.

Reflection

We have talked about how to leverage the power of the team, from selecting it to developing and coaching it. It is time to reflect.

- How do you select your team?
- Have you chosen the right person for each task?
- Do you know what motivates each of your team members? How do you align their personal ambitions to their actual contribution to the common goal?
- How do you embrace diversity? How do you benefit from the richness of diversity and energy of incorporating new talent?
- Which examples do you have of empowerment and learning from failures? Do you provide the empowerment you always wanted to have?

CHAPTER V

BUILD CUSTOMER OBSESSION

Those who know me would understand that this is one of my favourite chapters of this book. I love working with and for customers. Any business exists for one reason: its customers. They should be at the centre of everything you do. I learned how easy it is to forget it when you get caught up in the corporate dynamic.

Working with customers, you need to use all three dimensions. Sometimes combined, sometimes in isolation, and at the same time, you need to make sure that everybody in the organisation understands the impact they have on customers. Start by declaring the customer focus internally. Then follow up with clear actions to back up your words.

The Chief Engagement Officer must be the strongest customer advocate in the organisation. Customers sustain any business; they decide whether or not you will continue to be in post. Your company's success depends on their buying choices. If you work in a public function, citizens are your customers; their vote decides whether or not you will remain in post. All successful companies are obsessed with delivering for customers. You must make customers visible internally, lead by example, foster the attitude in the team, be prepared to learn from customers, and inspire and be inspired by them.

Make customers visible internally

Sales and service teams interact regularly with customers. But for internal functions it is harder, and they do not always have a good understanding what matters to them. We often talk about 'internal customers'; I hate this. The customer is the customer: the person, or entity, that consumes your products and services. The person, or entity, that pays, and sustains your business.

When I first became CEO, I found a team that was focused on zero defects. It was a well-thought out set of processes, with the goal to make no mistakes; to make sure that each department was serving the next one in the chain without failure. The 'internal customer' should be happy, and so the high level of internal quality was paramount. However, when talking to customers, they said we were far too slow and rigid. We were losing business because we had lost the customer's perspective. We tackled the issue by simplifying tasks, removing duplicated checks, creating parallel processes, and making sure the customer experience was the focus of every conversation in the company. We banned the idea that a finance person's customer was the internal unit they supported. We started to share what our customers were buying from us, and the importance of every role to make it happen.

This visibility and external focus must be in every action the CEO takes. There is a natural trend, especially in large organisations, to look inward. There is always the risk that people think the company is a self-sustained entity, and forget that everything should include the customer perspective.

A team that understands their role and how a satisfied customer will make your business better has a greater chance of success.

Every morning I would go to Coco di Mama, my favourite coffee shop close to our office in London's St. Paul's. I was a loyal customer for good reasons: they made a great skinny cappuccino, they remembered my name, and their team were always smiling, ready to wish you a great day. Daniel, the owner, told me one day that his approach was basic: they are, for many people, their first human interaction of the day. Their purpose is to try to make that experience a nice one. They want every customer to leave the shop happier than when they arrived because of the friendly spirit they create. It is a basic business principle but it works. You don't need to run a large global organisation to drive customer obsession.

It is important to build that sensitivity to customers across the organisation. You can make it visible in different moments. Keeping your message consistent is key. In order to keep the customer focus in everything a company does, you need to make it explicit every day.

As in any organisation, we often brought people together – for events, training courses, etc. I once went to a training session about collaboration, to provide the perspective of 'the boss'. I shared my 'view from the top' and at the end I asked: "Who do you think pays for this event?" Of course, I got the 'brown nose' answer: "You do, Luis." I smiled. Clearly not. "Human resources," other voices whispered. I shook my head. Finally, a shy voice offered: "Our customers." I nodded. Our customers pay for everything we do. They give us money in exchange for our products and services. So, when we spend it, we must keep them in mind. We should be confident in the knowledge that if they were a fly on the wall watching what we did with their money, they would still be happy to pay for our services.

To drive this consistent customer obsession, you must constantly remind people about what it is to serve your customers. I have found that the best way is sharing what you do for them through stories.

We decided that the easiest way to show what we do for our customers was to create a daily bulletin called 'the deal of the day'. It had to be a simple message, easy to read, covering what we had sold to the customer, and why we were able to win it, and so it became a learning opportunity for everybody. Each message should educate and inspire people about what we do, and recognise our success across different sectors and regions. When I began this, I did not realise the level of commitment it would need. But we did it for 10 years without fail – around 2,500 deals – and it was a clear success. I must say that I am proud of the different teams who made it happen and I particularly enjoyed the fact that at 8am every morning everyone in the business had the opportunity to read about 'the deal of the day'.

There is nothing like meeting customers in person. We made a point of inviting customers to our internal events, both face-to-face and by pre-recorded video. Of course, face-to-face gives a stronger message. It shows a high level of commitment and engagement if they are prepared to spend time with your team, thanking them for what they do well, and educating them on what they need to do better.

During one event, we asked three customers to take to the stage and share with us their perspectives of our company. Nationwide, DHL and British American Tobacco were on the panel in front of our senior management team. We learned about their business and challenges: a financial services organisation reinventing themselves and making technology a differentiator; a logistics company transforming to face the challenges of a more digital world; and a tobacco company creating a new business through e-cigarettes. We asked them how they were using our services to support their operations, and it helped us understand just how critical technology and connectivity has become for companies.

For those who were less familiar with our role as an extension of their businesses, it was an eye-opening moment. It finished with them telling us about what we did well, and how we could do better. Of course, you could always read surveys or case studies, but nothing compares with having the person, the customer, in front of us sharing their views and inspiring the team to be a better one. I decided that we should always have a customer section in our events.

Lead by example

Leading by example means spending quality time with customers, and showing that customer obsession is not always about saying yes.

As the leader of the team, you will demonstrate the importance of customers by the amount and quality of time you dedicate to them. Having customer meetings in your schedule is one clear example that will be highly visible to everybody. For example, whenever I travelled, I always made sure I spent the largest proportion of my time with customers. Whether it was an individual meeting, or a session with a group, they were always the biggest piece of the schedule. In fact, it was one of the main reasons for travelling in the first place – although whenever I had a trip I usually combined customers, the team and eventually external stakeholders, like analysts or the press. Depending on your business, the equivalent might be meeting channel partners or small customer focus groups. Whoever represents the voice of your customer should be a priority in your schedule.

Visiting customers at their premises allows you to understand the environment in which they operate, their core business, and how they embed technology within their operations. I remember my first visit to the Fiat factory in Belo Horizonte in Brazil. Their main office is on a mountaintop, and their factory is at the other end of the city. They were one of the largest car factories in the country. Engineers there regularly connected with the ones in Torino in Italy to discuss manufacturing issues or new elements to be considered. That connection was key. I met our team there, who were proud to work for Fiat – they felt as though they were part of the value chain for the customer. I could understand the importance of our role in keeping the factory running. It made me feel proud.

If you plan them well, these regional visits can help to reinforce your relationships with the customer's central departments. Just make a call or drop a message to your normal counterpart within the customer's organisation, explaining that you are visiting a new city, and you plan to meet their local team. Most importantly, ask whether there are any messages they would like you to convey, to help their global strategy. To customers in the field, it is good to meet global suppliers as it gives them the confidence in true partnership. You are acting in collaboration across units to balance the global-local relationship.

The quality of your meetings is reflected in clear outcomes. Always go to them well prepared. Define what they are for, whether it's for a catch up to find out how you are doing, or for a difficult negotiation. Your visibility is important. Your involvement is definitive.

Put yourself all in

By this, I mean make sure you are 100% with your customers when you meet them. You should also make sure that those client meetings help your team in front of the customer. On many occasions I would refer to the account manager as our boss. It may sound unusual, but it empowers your team and demonstrates that power to the customer. Otherwise, customers may just want to talk to you, and escalate to the CEO more frequently. The best sales and service people will be able to use you as a key resource when it comes to dealing with their account.

One day, I received a call from our team in Germany. They were in the final negotiations with a leading global chemical company. It had been a long process of discussions. In some moments, when it looked like something had been agreed, there had been small changes that put the whole deal at risk. The team were in the final steps, just a few critical points away from closing. We agreed that it would be worth me attending that closure meeting. My presence would show the customer that they were important to us, but it would also avoid any further delays on either side.

We started the meeting early in the morning, and we went back and forth over a few clauses. By early afternoon, everything was almost ready, and my flight home was just a couple of hours away. But both teams agreed to review the text again, so I said I would not leave until we had finalised the text, in the room, to avoid additional misinterpretation. It was a tense moment. It was not that I did not trust the team; in fact, it was the opposite. With all the relevant stakeholders in the room, it would be harder for the customer – or our team – to stall, re-open old queries, or try to make new interpretations of any items. We spent the next hour writing down the final version – and I even made my flight on time. I learned that sometimes your presence could help your team, not just by demonstrating the importance of the customer but also backing their position in a negotiation.

And you build relationships that last for a long time. Recently, I had an inspiring conversation with a customer who reminded me of the meeting we had had in Singapore 12 years earlier. Back then, we had shared the challenges we faced as CIOs, and he told me that discussion had helped him with his own role. Being able to help a customer without selling them anything is priceless.

When you are in a business-to-business environment, your personal commitment is highly visible. Having direct access to the CEO is reassuring for customers. But not because they want a direct conversation with him every day; it shows he is interested in them, he will be on top of their service, and he will be ready to support them with their own bosses. You can make a small gesture, like including your personal mobile number on your business card. I did it during all my years as CEO and I didn't receive one call that was not worth it. And the customers knew they could contact me if needed.

There are many ways to set the example of customer obsession for your team.

We were visting our operation in Brussels. In the afternoon, we met with customers at an event jointly organised with the British Embassy. We shared our experience around the 2012 Olympics and the evolution of the business. The best moments were the individual conversations with customers. There were many of them, and it was a great opportunity for us to spend quality time with them.

I talked to NATO and European Union Institutions representatives, as well as others like Euroclear and Ideal Standard. We listened to their challenges, and explained our views of the industry and our approach to supporting them with innovative solutions.

At the end of the event, the organiser was arranging transport back to our hotel and he asked:" Luis, when will you leave?" I replied: "When the last customer leaves."

Let me explain why I said it. Of course, I was tired after a long journey, but I consider time to be the second most valuable asset we have after our health. If people with very busy schedules are prepared to spend time with us, we should recognise it and, at least, be there while they are. Doing otherwise is like organising a great dinner at your home and when you reach dessert, telling your guests: "Well, I am going to bed. Enjoy the rest of the evening."

Learn to say no

Being available to customers, being personally involved in discussions and loving to work with them is not everything. A customer wants to have an honest relationship in exchange for their confidence. Your ambition should be to become a real trusted advisor. In customer relationships, there is a risk that you do not share openly what you think. You could become a slave to the connection.

Because one of the most difficult, but necessary, conversations is when you disagree with your customer. Someone once told me: "If our customers go to the moon, we will go to the moon." This was their way of reflecting that their business should be customer centric. But what it does not mean is that you should do whatever your customers ask for.

This is controversial for some people but, personally, it is a key leadership differentiator. You must be ready to tell the truth, even if you will lose your business. Providing an honest view will foster the debate with the customer. It is also the meaning of the word 'partnership'. Any great services company should have in its DNA the determination to come back to the customer with their view. And customers prefer that, even if they don't often express it. They trust you and expect you to be honest with them.

Listening to customers is a key skill when it comes to doing better business. Sometimes we try too hard to please customers, thinking this is what they want. But most customers expect to be challenged when they ask for a specific service or solution. They see your organisation as the expert. They want advice, not just acceptance.

We faced a challenging situation when a large European player issued a Request for Proposal for a significant transformation of their infrastructure. We reviewed what they wanted to do in detail. We thought it was an expensive solution and difficult to implement. In our opinion, it was not going to solve their problems. So, we tried to explain why we believed it was not the right choice. They did not budge, so we wrote a letter declining our participation. It was a difficult decision. But you should stick to your principles and knowledge. It was impossible to provide what they wanted within a reasonable price and solution.

Of course, the team felt frustrated as they had worked hard to get into that account. I told them: "Our customers are highly demanding. They want us to perform to our best to meet their expectations. Athletes who compete among the best face situations in which they win, and others in which they lose. One of the most difficult lessons in elite sport is how to manage defeat."

I had a call with this customer's CIO and their Chief Procurement Officer, and they told me officially that we were totally out of the process as a consequence of our letter. It was not easy to digest. The closer and harder you work on a deal, the more difficult it is to accept losing it.

However, these are great moments to understand who you are as a team and as a company. First, we learned the importance of resilience, especially when facing defeat. Customers value it when you don't give up easily. Second, we felt the pride of being part of the team. They showed what it meant to be a team: fighting for the same objective, leveraging each other's strengths, working long hours together, and supporting each other. The offer we worked on was not just a set of files. It was our joint belief in our capabilities, our joint passion to serve our customers, and our joint ambition to win and to lead the market.

Interestingly, around six months later, we received a call from the customer. When they reviewed our competitors' offers, they realised we were right. No one could provide what they were asking for, and those who were close had an astronomical cost.

I flew over to discuss a more sensible design with the team and the customer. We then worked hard to present an updated offer, and at the end of the process we won a significant part of their infrastructure.

Personally, I learned a lot in those months, working hard to gain the confidence of the customer. I learned about the quality of the people and how the joint work of sales, technical, commercial and legal teams can create unbeatable offers. I also learned about the importance of being close to customers, listening to their needs, and performing beyond expectations. But even more importantly, the value of being honest, even at the risk of losing business.

Develop the art of working with customers

Customers want to buy from winning companies. I notice it as a consumer. I like to buy from exciting and prosperous brands. I have also witnessed it while working with businesses. The team in front of the customer should feel and act as a winning team. They should be proud of the company they work for, and its products and solutions. They should smile because they are proud to be part of such a successful organisation. The service units should also feel proud, regardless of how big a problem they're facing. You must create this spirit and attitude because it will be highly visible to your clients. That pride should be based on what you do for your customers and the society.

Collaborate to serve global customers

When you work for a global company, you typically refer to your customers as global accounts. This means they are served globally as one account, regardless of how many subsidiaries or regional divisions it has. Managing a global account is a key practice for any global player but it is also a very challenging one.

First, you must identify where the decisions are made and where the budget sits. Some expenses can be decided regionally but others are central. Trying to sell a solution into a country unit could be a big mistake and affect the whole relationship with the client. On one occasion, we were trying to sell to a global pharmaceutical company. In this case, they had a centralised budget for the telecommunications infrastructure. However, the decision committee had representatives from all regions. So, it was important to build relationships with the local teams to improve their confidence in us, even though they would not make the end decision.

Next, you must understand the global strategies they are implementing. In this example, the Global Chief Information Officer was putting in place a shared global logistics platform. He needed all units around the globe to adopt it. Hence, he wanted all the suppliers to reinforce his message and not to offer alternative solutions to individual countries.

You must also balance the global and the local presence. A strong centralised relationship is necessary. However, by connecting with the local teams, you can impact the global strategy and, at the same time, have access to some local business. In this example, there was local budget for a voice solution, for which you needed to have presence in the country. We won because we had the capability.

Drive your team with discipline and define incentives that foster collaboration. Conflicting sales targets can drive the wrong behaviours and impact the customer. The sales objectives should recognise the global presence as well as local targets. At the beginning, we did not spend enough time on this, so our teams were not aligned enough.

Finally, you should also make sure you follow your customers' evolution. A global company might change their structure over time, so you must be flexible to adjust to it. A few times, we made the mistake of trying to impose our management models without listening properly to customers. For example, one customer decided to devolve budget decisions to their regional units, and so they wanted local contacts. We had a centralised team at the time, so we reorganised our team too to cover their new way of working.

Listen to customers; it is the best sales tool you have

We mentioned that the Chief Engagement Officer should listen internally to the team. This also applies to customers. Those listening skills can become your best tool to sell more, and sell better. By making this part of the DNA of your organisation, you will find more business opportunities and you will be able to respond faster and more precisely to customer needs. We are surrounded by information telling us what could be a new prospect. We just need to process it. Being curious and continuously asking your customer questions will make you wiser about their business and their challenges.

In one of our sales conferences, in Den Hague, I hosted a round table with sales directors from across Europe. One of them was managing sales people who were struggling to find deals. He told them: "You can look at a newspaper as a list of news, or you can read it as an inventory of new business opportunities. A merger or acquisition, a restructuring plan or an organisation entering a new market represents a unique moment of opportunity to trigger an interaction with the customer. Make sure you follow the top executives on social media, as well as key people within your customer's organisation. It will allow you to have a fresh interaction and know what currently matters to them."

It is all about understanding what you can do to contribute to your customer's life or business. I like the concept of customer journeys as the lifecycle of the relationship between a customer and your business. The business-to-business market has a different way of looking at journeys, as there is a different way of interacting in the process. I once heard a very good sales guy talking about his job: "I don't have targets, I have dreams. I don't have customers, I have relationships." Those relationships are built across the whole journey and over several years and iterations. You must be open to opportunities.

I particularly enjoy the tale about two shoe salesmen who travel to a remote place in search of new business opportunities. When they arrive, they notice that nobody was wearing shoes. One man calls base home and says: "I'm coming back home. There's no hope here. Nobody here is wearing shoes, so there's no one to sell to." The second man calls home and says: "You won't believe what I found here. There is so much opportunity. No one here is wearing shoes. I can sell to the whole country!"

Create business opportunities

It is all about attitude and you can create that around you. When you read an article relating to a customer, send the link to the sales team. If you find a tweet or a post from a CEO sharing their new ambitions, work out how you can help him. Leading by example is the easiest way to drive a cultural change. Call customers, send them an email, and congratulate them or offer help. Whether it is a significant security issue or just a new acquisition, being aware and reacting is your best way of winning their confidence as it shows you care.

I experienced this when I was CEO of one of our operations, and we acquired a company specialising in Cloud services. It was published in the news and we got good recognition as it complemented our capabilities. On the same day it was in the news, I got an email from a consulting company: 'Luis, congratulations on your acquisition. Let us know if we can help.' The following day I got a call from one of their competitors, who said: "Luis, congratulations, we have seen the news. As you know, we are here to support you. We know the sector well and we think there are good opportunities to grow and drive efficiencies. If there is anything we can do to help, let us know."

I got a longer email a few days later from a third company: 'Luis, we saw your acquisition and we think it is a very good one. We have registered ourselves as a customer for both your service and theirs, and we have made a comparison. We have also explored your customers and theirs, and we have created a list of potential cross-selling opportunities. So, based on what we know, we have a proposal for a plan of synergies. We would love to sit with you and your team to go through these three areas if it works for you.' You can imagine, as a customer, how the three different approaches landed, and you can guess which company we ended up working with. I learned about the following three attitudes that I valued in the last approach.

First, interest in the business of your customer. You go beyond the news. You explore the actual opportunity, you are curious and you walk the talk. You use your knowledge of the market.

Second, hunger. You show your eagerness to work together by being proactive, by doing instead of waiting to be told. You are ready to take the risk of proposing. You even become a customer to learn. You do the unexpected.

Third, action. You create a plan and create an opportunity. You are in the driving seat. You generate trust that you are ready to lead if that is needed.

To do what they did is all about attitude. Willingness, appetite and ambition – this is what makes a difference in any business. Going that extra mile for the customer may not cost a lot but it means a lot.

Pay attention to small things that really count

You can complement that attitude with small but meaningful gestures. Small things count in life. When it comes to customer experience, they are just as important as the big things. Your customers recognise when you care, and you can show it vividly with small signals.

I went to Clairmont Ferrand to review the rollout of a contract with Michelin. I was really impressed by the way our team were working together with the client network manager. The customer explained how trivial things complemented a well-managed and well-executed migration of services. He highlighted actions like calling local managers in advance to tell them about a date of change, calling afterwards just to say thank you, or keeping them updated on new technological developments that could benefit them. They were pleased that when our team found new, even tiny, saving oportunities, they were telling the customer and implementing quickly.

I felt inspired when listening to how you can make a big impact with small actions at the same time as implementing large transformational projects.

Learn from customers

The next step in creating this customer obsession is learning. Once you have listened, use what you have heard to develop patterns that will make your organisation a better one. It is about cultivating corporate knowledge based on your experience. You should understand why you win and why you lose, you should continuously ask what you could do better, and you should measure service quality to learn how you can make it a differentiator.

Ask "what can we do better?"

Meeting customers is always an opportunity, whether it is for a courtesy visit, a relevant service issue or a business discussion. In every single opportunity, I always asked the same question: "What can we do better?" Negative questions like: "What do we do badly?" or "What don't you like about us?" put the customer in a difficult situation. They prefer to be in positive territory with constructive comments, and you will welcome those reflections from them.

When I met the CIO of a pharmaceutical company, we were there to discuss the services we were implementing for them. It was a complex solution that was taking more time than expected. I knew the challenges we were facing. However, I still decided to ask the question: "What can we do better?" His answer was eye opening for me: "You should have challenged us more. I believe that some of our problems are down to the fact that you were not bold enough with us in the design phase. We expect you to be our advisor. You can be better at that."

I found this question to be one of the best ways to get customer feedback. It turns the conversation into a progressive discussion looking more for improvements, rather than focusing on issues. There may seem to be little difference between the phrases "Your billing is not good" and "You must improve your billing." But the second phrase puts your organisation into action mode, rather than dwelling on the problem.

These individual conversations are very useful and your Engagement side should encourage you to have as many of these as possible. However, to capture opinion from a wider population, you must put in place a proper systematic process. Net Promoter Score (NPS) systems are being used more and more in the market. It is a management tool to measure customer loyalty, complementary to other customer satisfaction metrics. It is a simple, powerful way of aligning your organisation. It asks the customer to rate on a scale from 1-10 how likely you are to recommend the company. Those rating 9 and 10 are considered promoters, 7 and 8 are neutral, and 6 and below are detractors.

When we were planning to implement NPS I was a bit sceptical that with a single metric we could achieve a stronger customer focus. We started by cleaning the customer list to be interviewed, counting the number of messages sent and answered, and of course looking at the actual results. We held a weekly meeting with the top sales and service representatives to review what we had learned. We looked at overall outcomes and individual customer specifics. In less than six months, NPS became common language, a collective way of looking at how well we were doing for customers. Our score improved by more than 11 points in the first year, with even better progress in customers with repeated surveys. Service should be the highest priority in any organisation. However, I found it difficult to measure a customer's actual level of happiness with the service we provide. NPS helped us. I learned, once again, the power of consistency to drive solid results.

Put service at the heart of your team

Creating a culture of service requires something beyond an intellectual understanding of what it means for customers. There is also an emotional element to it. The reason people will go above and beyond their day job is an inner sense of responsibility. It reflects that they care about their customers, and how their activities could be impacted by a failure or a delay. Even in a corporate world you deal with people. You meet and work with professionals who are trying to do their best, and who run businesses with a high impact on society. Whether it is a consumer goods company, a logistics player or a bank, what they do should matter to your team, and this is where the personal commitment comes in.

I remember a discussion with the Customer Service Director, a few weeks after he took his job. I asked him how it was going. He gave me a comprehensive view of the transformation they were driving. His main focus areas for improvement were delivering complex projects, resourcing and efficiency.

But he also said that the thing he found most unexpected was understanding how critical we were for our customers. "The level of dependency on their services and operations is high, and hence our responsibility grows, as an extension of their business. It gives me a sense of pride that makes our job so special. But when we fail them, it really hurts." And he pointed to his stomach when he said it, and he really meant it.

I am sure most of you share, as I do, the same feeling when you fail your customers. It is this passion to serve that also makes the team keep doing amazing things for them. In any service organisation, this is what you expect from the team. It is about caring, understanding and feeling the service beyond the figures of service level agreements.

Learn why you win and why you lose

Learning how to enhance service should become a continuous task across the organisation and you should take a similar approach in sales-related activities. In this case, you must understand why you win and why you lose.

You might recognise success as the value of the contracts you have signed, or if you are in a corporate business-to-business market, as the brand names you win. You usually ask sales teams about how they did it and what lessons they learned. So you should also analyse why you lose. Interestingly, most organisations would say they win due to the 'customer relationship', and they lose due to a lack of 'price competitiveness'. As a salesman, I find this to be an easy answer that mediocre sales people would give. It lacks proper insights into the real reasons why something has happened.

Understanding the reasons why you win and lose is, to me, the essence of becoming a leader in the market. The more granular the analysis you can make about it, the better insights you will get, and therefore you will be able to give better offers, use your resource better, and win more.

Prepare to win

Winning means that you have signed a contract with the right level of returns, and a good understanding of your commitment and the risks associated with what you have agreed. These three elements – profit, service and risks – are the basics of good business practices. I used to be on the buying side, as Head of Procurement, when I was running IT for a large bank. When you buy, you never know how low you could have pushed your supplier. You do not know the margins. But you can compare with other suppliers to make sure you are buying at a fair level. When you sell, you can – and have to – know your margins. This is a key metric for your sales people. They should own it, be rewarded by it and make it part of their expertise in negotiating and making trade-offs.

I always asked the same set of questions to our sales people: Do we have a view of the winning price? Do we understand what the customer's expectations are, or how much they are willing to spend? Do we have a view of their actual costs and the levels of savings they wish to make?

If you can understand the dynamic of what the customer is looking for, then you can have that as the basis of your proposal. The requirements are a key component as they determine your costs. This may sound like an obvious and even stupid statement but it is important. I have found occasions in which we have included elements in a proposal that were not really what the customer wanted, and that increased our costs. In other cases, when you talked to the customer about what is or is not standard, customers were ready to trade.

In summary, the key element to winning is the actual willingness to gain the deal. It means understanding what the customer is aiming for, spending time and effort on the quality of the solution and your ability to deliver it, and making sure you make money using the right level of resources. The best deals I have signed had those three components established early in the process.

Know why you lose

Winning is great, but we often face defeat too. It took me a while to realise it, but you learn more from losses than from wins. I found it frustrating reviewing deals we lost. It could be easy to say: "We were not well prepared" or "We did not know the customer well enough." Those can be indicators; however, they are not the core reasons why you lose. Don't have a light discussion if you want to learn. Do a deep dive, ask the 'five whys' until you understand.

There are three fundamental groups of root causes:

- You did not capture what the customer wanted well enough. So, how are you going to improve this knowledge for future opportunities?

- Your product or solutions design was not fit for purpose in terms of the features needed. Are those characteristics part of the development roadmap? If not, why not?

- Your offer was too expensive. Did we overcomplicate the design? Are our costs not competitive enough?

A few years ago, we were preparing a response to the European RFP for a tyres manufacturer. We did not have a meaningful relationship with the customer, but their requirements were at the core of our capabilities. So, we presented it. But after some discussions, we lost. We requested a session to understand why, and this helped us to learn more about the customer's priorities, elements of our solution that were too complicated, and some price issues. The customer continued to finalise negotiations with their selected supplier. But we told them that, given our new insight, we would refine our offer in case they needed us. It was time and money well spent as we learned a lot in the process. Our country manager explained that we were there for a long-term relationship and not just for a deal. Therefore, we wanted to learn and keep in touch.

A few weeks later, they called us. They were not happy with how their conversations had progressed, and they were ready to engage with us. This time we were better prepared, and after a month we signed the contract with them. By learning why you lose, you can prepare to win if you don't give up.

Inspire and be inspired by customers

The highest level of engagement in a customer-obsessed organisation is inspiring and being inspired. To get to this level, you should have the basics right: excellent service, right prices and solid relationships. To build this strong connection with your clients, you must create inspiring moments of engagement, understand innovation plans in your customer's business, and drive innovation in your solutions.

In a business-to-business environment, trust is a necessary element of the commercial relationship. You can achieve good engagement with customers by creating special moments in which you connect beyond the operational links.

One of my most inspiring experiences happened around the 2012 Olympics.

More than 4 billion people watched the London 2012 Olympics, thanks to the technologies our company provided, and the largest ever variety of devices, from HD TV to smartphones. Two hundred and five national teams participated in those 30th Olympic Games of modern history. Walking through the streets of London that summer you could feel the Olympic spirit, with thousands of flags from almost all the countries around the globe. For us, this was the best showcase we could ever dream of to demonstrate our capabilities to our customers: delivering and managing complex and critical networks. Our team delivered 'the most connected Games ever' at the time. We wanted to be highly visible during such an inspiring event. 'Inspire a generation' was one of our themes.

We organised some events to demonstrate this to dozens of customers from around the world. We started with an explanation of our contribution to the infrastructure across the Olympic venues: about 80,000 connections in 94 locations, 1,800 wireless access points and 16,500 telephone lines. We provided high-speed broadband connections and wifi to the 14,700 athletes, and more 60 Gb/s were available to transmit the incredible amount of information being shared and distributed by journalists, but also by all participants and spectators.

We also had a session with Ade Adepitan, a silver medal Paralympics basketball player from Team GB (Great Britain Olympics team). Ade explained how, when he was 11, he dreamed of being an Olympic athlete, but having contracted polio, his dream seemed an impossible one. However, after overcoming many difficult experiences, he has proved that aiming for the impossible was worth it. That made me wonder how many times we find barriers in front of us, disabling us from realising our dreams. And I thought about how one can overcome these barriers, whatever they are, by focusing on what you want to achieve instead of focusing on what makes it impossible to achieve it.

Our customers were impressed and inspired. The CEO of the group at the time came to welcome them. In such an inspiring environment, business conversations flew with a different tone. We discussed innovation and future oportunities to collaborate.

With an indirect partner from Japan, we agreed to do more for Japanese companies based in Europe. The CIO of a bank asked us to help them reduce their cost base by using more technology in their operations, so many others wanted to leverage our experience.

Those informal discussions were happening alongside the different events, transfers, meals and relaxed moments used to refresh after long walks. It was a fantastic occasion, not to be missed. Customers appreciated those chances to be inspired, and we combined those messages with the evolution of our technology offerings. I learned how important it is to build those moments to improve engagement and gain credibility.

Understand customer innovation challenges

Customers are also ready to share what motivates them and how their industry evolves. They face challenges created by disruptive technologies and new business models. Realising those challenges is fundamental for your business and how you support your clients. Always be curious and use any chance you have to learn about that in a conversation or, even better, visiting a factory, a shop or a branch. Those conversations with customers always inspire me. When they share how they confront those risks and opportunities, they provide a perspective that you can extrapolate to your own business. Even more importantly, by understanding how they think and transform, you can build better services for them.

Yara is a leading global fertiliser manufacturer. They provide solutions for agriculture and the environment. Their CIO attended one of our customer events and shared their ambition to embrace digital technologies. You could consider agriculture to be a traditional industry where digital innovation is less relevant than in others. He described to us how they have acquired a few companies specialising in sensors. For several years, Yara has invested in R&D and innovation to convert crop-based agronomy and application knowledge into a digital format, through the development of precision farming tools and services.

Understanding Yara's determination to move into digital services helped us to propose new services that would better manage the infrastructure underneath their new solutions.

This is just one example of the many customers we learned about every day. You should make the time to go through these transformations in your customers' operating models. I learned as much or even more from those conversations than from internal meetings about new ideas. Sometimes, I felt overwhelmed by the level of innovation they were driving. We talk a lot about startups and inventions, but I realised how big companies are also taking seriously what the digital revolution means for them.

Innovation is also a broad topic. There is innovation in new technologies, innovation in the way you apply old technologies in a different way, and innovation in commercial models. You can also find cases that combine all three. The use of, for example, advanced AI (artificial intelligence) techniques is possible because of the evolution of software and hardware solutions. The availability of cheaper and wider platforms allows companies to manage data on a larger scale. It is called 'big data'. By deploying it, you can learn about consumers' behaviours. You can then make offers based on the location of those customers and create a new business out of it for retailers. The possibilities are endless. The challenge you face as a supplier is to be able to inspire your customers.

Several years ago, we decided to include an innovation clause in customer contracts. This was to demonstrate our commitment to bringing new ideas and services to the table. We arranged quarterly sessions in which we openly discussed our developments and investments in R&D. We also brought external perspectives of what was happening in the market, in our customers' industries and in others. We examined market trends and exchanged views about them. On some occasions, we hosted those innovation sessions in our research laboratories. We sometimes agreed to make a proof of concept or run a pilot. In most instances, we co-funded it and in some cases, we even ended up with a new product in the market.

A large fashion firm wanted to improve their efficiency in the way they operated around the globe. They had teams spread across Hong Kong, New York, Amsterdam and Paris that worked together to design new clothes for the next season. One of their challenges was getting everyone together despite such distances. Travelling was expensive in both time and money. At that time, we had launched a high-definition videoconference service. The Telepresence service, as it was called, delivered excellent quality images and sound. Telepresence rooms in each location had the same layout and decoration, so it gave the impression of being in the same room. After a few minutes, people became immersed in the discussion in such a way that collaboration was very effective.

The project functioned very well. Designers shared textiles, colours and buttons, and they had models in different locations trying on dresses. We ended up calling it the virtual dressing room. I was impressed how fast joint innovation discussions resulted in a solution like that.

Reflection

We have discussed the role of the Chief Engagement Officer when it comes to building customer obsession. It is time to reflect.

- How do you make the voice of the customer heard in your organisation?

- What can you do to make the customer more visible to everybody, regardless of their role?

- How do you lead by example?

- Think of examples where a turnaround of a customer issue has become an opportunity to improve the relationship and check if it has been transformed into corporate knowledge.

- What are your sources of inspiration about your customer's business changes? How do you follow their transformation and how you can help them?

- How do you take the lessons learned from winning and losing business?

- Consider examples of joint innovation with customers in your organisation or in other sectors. What can you learn from those?

CHAPTER VII

DRIVE HIGH PERFORMANCE

Between Evangelism and Engagement, the CEO has set the framework. He has defined the vision and knows what he wants to achieve. The team is ready to make it happen and the customers are aligned to support the company. You might have noticed the clear interrelation of both dimensions. The basis for any communication is knowing the destination. The stronger the interaction with the different communities, the better the vision will be supported and refined. These two dimensions should be balanced and, depending on the situation, one will be more visible than the other. However, both will always be present. Now it is time to enter the Execution dimension.

The Chief Execution Officer is responsible for translating the vision into plans and following their implementation with determination. He should drive forward a high-performance organisation. He should keep focus, to avoid damaging distractions. He should enforce change, becoming the leading change agent of the organisation. Those elements will guarantee a flawless execution to make the vision come true. In this process, engaging the people is also critical, to complete the actions required in each phase. This is where the three dimensions play together at their best. I found that it requires full attention to balance them properly. By mastering that balance, you will become a stronger leader.

Success is linked to performance. In any sport discipline, the better you perform, the higher the satisfaction, pride and eventually recognition. That is success. High performance focus starts with defining expectations of what you intend to achieve. Then, it is essential to outline how performance will be tracked, build a proper set of metrics, and consistently evaluate them. You should leverage the power of the organisation by fostering cross-fertilisation of best practices. A high-performance team should be at the core of any great company, and you can build it.

Define clear expectations

Brilliant execution requires solid planning. It means taking the vision to the next level of detail. It is about making sure that everybody knows what he or she needs to do. So you need to be clear on your expectations, use target setting well to drive performance, and create a culture of attention to detail.

Explain how you work

I found that as well as describing what to do, it is important to share how you want people to act. Your team should know what to expect from you, and what you expect from them. By explaining how you operate, you will make it easier for people to work with you, and it will make conversations and meetings more effective.

When I started as CEO, the head of communications asked me: "How do you work?" I was surprised. "What do you mean?" I asked. She meant what were my rules of engagement, of addressing problems, of discussing issues or taking decisions. She said: "For those who do not know you, it will be easier if you articulate your principles of operation." So, we put them in writing. At first I was not sure how useful it would be. But it saved me a lot of time and energy in the long run. Those very basic principles helped people to understand my leadership style. If you share them early on, you can refer to them in your day-to-day meetings and conversations. They were as follows:

I don't like surprises. Financial analysts, customers and people alike appreciate predictability. It allows them to make financial models, plan and execute accordingly. An unpredictable business creates uncertainty, which is the hardest enemy when it comes to securing funding and trust. By anticipating issues, you could prevent risks. So, everybody should be prepared to raise issues and concerns, as well as good news. A great new deal could require more resources and investments, which you need to plan for. Surprises limit your ability to deal with them. Knowing in advance that something could happen will allow you to prepare properly. It also means that people should be ready to ask for help. When someone identifies a problem, it should be raised. It does not matter whose responsibility it is. Sharing the problem means you are forced to articulate the issue well, present the plan to resolve it, assess the risk, and be prepared to receive advice and help to improve the solution. In summary, it is making risk management a key skill of your organisation.

Our customers pay for everything we do. I have already referred to this. However, it means that customers must be really at the centre of everything we do. Our business is built for them; they recognise our value and are prepared to pay for it. This should be reflected in the way we spend time and money – on events, trips, resources, training, or third parties. You should always question the real need of doing something – is it a 'nice to have' or a necessity? Listen to the voice of the customer in everything you do. Doing a sort of 'customer check' for your decisions will provide a very valid angle.

As a team, we discuss solutions, not problems. You may recognise this situation. A friend of mine calls it 'admiring the problem'. Spending time on the details of a particular challenge is good if it is done with a view to finding the solution. But I have attended several meetings in which the problem was the king – it was chairing the session, and we were all huddled around that problem. In some cases, it was not even a well-defined issue. Shift the focus. Don't look at the problem, tackle it. You can make a difference by asking the right questions and steering the discussion to a productive place. I was amazed to watch the whole organisation change over time, just by keeping this discipline of jointly looking at solutions.

We don't just ask our people to deliver; we ask them what they need to deliver. There are references to this in different chapters of this book. The role of a leader is to support a team, not just asking them to produce outcomes. The risk of just demanding is that it can create immediate disengagement. On the other hand, support must be associated with strong accountability to deliver, so that it is not used as an excuse for failure. This was part of my side of the contract with the team. I told them that if they found our requests unreasonable, we should discuss them. But the goal was to identify what was required to achieve the target, instead of giving up. It was all about how we could provide the necessary resources to execute the plans.

We are clear and honest. We share what we think openly and respectfully. Successful organisations are based on people who are able to be honest, and respect other people's views. A clear and honest conversation can identify wrong behaviours and allow them to be corrected. It can foster diversity, debate and get better results. Disagreement is a powerful improvement tool. Fear of expressing oneself is a blocker to growth. Sometimes it is not intentional; hence it requires good management attention. Ask people to speak up openly whenever you can. You can be the first stopper to people's openness. If you always share your opinions first, or if you instantly refute any opinions, you could discourage sincerity.

We are ambitious and always want more. This is the sporting spirit. Good is not enough. In a heavily competitive market, the bar is rising every year. You must become unreasonable. Customers expect you to keep improving. You must create that positive ambition to perform better. However, you must also be able to demonstrate and celebrate progress and success – otherwise you risk creating a permanently unsatisfied team.

Balance it by recognising improved results; this will encourage others to keep going as well.

In several meetings, I referred to this list of principles. We even published it to make it easier for people to understand how I operate, and what they can expect from me. I even remember the moment an operations manager told me: "Luis, I know you don't like surprises. There could be some issues tomorrow because there is a big change in the power supply for a large data centre. We have strong plans in place. However, this is significant enough for you to be aware. We will keep you posted." My team and their managers applied this small list of principles, and it became an informal management style guide.

Set clear targets

Setting targets is a cornerstone for driving performance. Targets should be aligned to the vision and the plans to implement it, and it is important to find a balance between targets, objectives and incentives. Targets are the quantitative results linked to key business indicators. Objectives are more qualitative outcomes. Incentives are the compensation schemes associated to objectives and targets. I found it useful to separate quantitative and qualitative goals, especially when conducting performance reviews.

When it comes to setting targets, I learned that there are certain risks to watch:

- Making every goal a team goal. It may appear to foster great teamwork, as people will support each other to achieve that common goal. But in my experience, team targets can dilute the personal accountability. The feeling of joint delivery should be complementary to the direct personal responsibility. A good balance of both drives the right behaviours.

- Confusing objectives and role descriptions. This is another frequent mistake. I had this discussion when reviewing a programme manager's targets. Initially, she had: 'organising meetings with a clear schedule and managing the time to have effective sessions'. Of course, any good programme manager should arrange the meetings properly. But that is their job description. So we agreed to change it to: 'by the end of the year, reduce the number of meetings and the time they consume by 20%, by driving them more efficiently'. This meant she was focused on a specific accomplishment. This will encourage change and improvement. That is what you want from a personal objective.

- Setting an unachievable target. There is a fine balance between challenge and discouragement. While you must avoid being demanding to the extent of appearing unreasonable, you should also be able to judge what makes sense. A well-defined ambition encourages people to do better. It encourages people to work together to improve. In sport, you will aspire to get a better time, to run faster or to lift a heavier weight. It is a way to motivate people. However, if you are asking someone to lift two tons, they will probably give up instead of focusing on beating their target. It can be difficult to judge the level of challenge. Make sure targets are fair.

- Misaligning targets between units. There will always be some tension when you set an ambition to reduce costs in one support unit and to grow resources in other. In our business, the Facilities Management unit had a target to reduce the use of space, whilst at the same time a business unit was growing their team and looking for more space. We resolved it by having a more sophisticated metric for the Facilities team: cost per employee. It removed the dependency on how many new employees were coming or going. At the same time, we targeted the expanding unit to limit its number of floors by using collaboration tools to encourage flexible working. A good method to reach alignment is to organise sessions where people share their goals, and ask them to find a way of making them compatible. They will show inconsistencies and they will trigger a healthy discussion. As a leader, it is worth dealing with the risk of disputes. Conflicting targets often generate a robust debate, but they can also waste time and energy.

- Establishing solid, well-structured targets, but not underpinning the main targets of your business. Take, for example, the targets for your training department. Employees could spend the right number of hours in courses, but they might not be the right courses. Someone must make sure that the focus on training is aligned to the core business. Your people could have wasted time in training for standard products, instead of new portfolio solutions. They could have spent time and money on face-to-face training where an online course would have done the job. These elements should be reflected in the targets. It is about doing the right things, not just doing things right.

In summary, setting targets is an essential tool to drive performance. What motivates your people is key. You should dedicate time to making sure that the organisation defines targets, objectives and incentives that support the vision. I have heard CEOs saying: "My direct team should know what they have to do. I don't need to define targets or objectives for them individually. They are grown-ups." I made that mistake once as well. But it is not just about the financial results or the key performance indicators. Everybody needs a clear, personal challenge, where they can demonstrate their contribution and progress.

I used to have revenue, profit and cash as core targets for my team, as well as a set of personal objectives. For example, the Director of Portfolio was targeted on market penetration in specific customer segments, customer loyalty improvements, and volunteering participation. Then, when setting incentives, her bonus was split between these personal goals and the overall results of the business. You foster collaboration by setting common goals, and you guarantee personal accountability through individual targets.

Achievement means different things in different companies. In one of our events, we had the head of Google's Cloud business as a presenter. We discussed challenging targets and compensation. He told us that 70% of their bonus was associated to individual targets, 20% was linked to the contribution they made to others' success, and the final 10% was linked to some out-of-the-box thinking or innovative projects. It showed, once again, how much you could drive performance, and guide where people spend time and effort by setting the right targets.

Pay attention to detail

Attention to detail is something I have always considered a differentiator in a leader. It is an intrinsic capability for a focused Chief Execution Officer. I learned the importance of knowing and understanding the details of your business. It means having a good view of the customers you have, the products they use, the margins you make, where expenses are, and how many people are working in any specific area. Being able to dive deep to the lowest possible level of detail has helped me to make sense of the big numbers and key parameters. The best leaders can explain a profit and loss account or the dynamic of their business in a very simple way. It means you need a deep understanding of every component.

Details count when you run any business. The CEO of Dixons was visiting some of their shops across the UK. She had only recently been appointed. She told me her ambition was to understand the business better, closer to their customers – and what better than those high street stores. She was walking through one branch with the store manager, and there was a piece of paper on the floor. They both saw it. She picked it up and put it in the bin. She explained to me that if you don't pay attention to every single detail, business would deteriorate. It is not good practice to think that you are too high in the organisation to pick up a piece of paper. I smiled; we had done something similar, tidying up the cables when visiting a data centre.

When looking at the detail, I found it extremely useful to break the business into pieces you can digest, understand and act on, whether it is customer segments, portfolio products, regions or operational costs elements. Then, by going deeper, you will understand the dynamics of each small component. It will help you to see interdependencies, and it will make it easier to make decisions.

We were scrutinising the structure of the cost of telecommunications. We split it into elements. One element was data lines. We broke this down into the kinds of lines, based on speeds, then by region, then by country, then by customer. It gave me a detailed view of where our expenses lay and where to focus. But that knowledge also made people aware of dependencies on suppliers and the lack of high bandwidth connections. It was an eye-opening exercise for everybody. I learned a lot about our business. Attention to detail will provide you with an invaluable perspective.

Track performance

Once you have clear ambitions, it is time to track how your business performs. To push powerful track performance, you must make sure you hold inspiring business reviews, create a can-do approach, and use paradoxical thinking, as we will discuss later, to improve the way people tackle problems.

Hold inspiring business reviews

In most organisations, there is a formal process to review business performance, from the lowest levels to the highest ranks of the company. I learned that, regardless of where you sit, there are some practices that can make them useful, practical and even inspiring.

The first reflection to make is: Where do you spend your time in those reviews? Are they looking back, or looking forward?

Business reviews offer you a unique learning opportunity. You can understand the business better, you can generate good discussions around future actions, and you can discover talent by interacting with the team. They can be inspiring moments for people.

You can use those evaluations to instil a way of working, a reflection on how to run operations.

In one of my first business reviews as CEO, I was with a regional unit and I explained how I look at business in those reviews: "There are three sets of figures I like to use when looking at performance: targets, results and forecasts."

In most businesses I know, there is an annual planning process in which you define what you aim to achieve in terms of results. This could be a financial result, or it could be an operational metric, like the number of cars sold, or mobile customers acquired. That is what I call the target, and there will be financial budgets associated with it. Personally, I always keep the target in mind. It was defined during the planning process. Maintaining it will facilitate your ability to plan longer term.

However, when you start executing the plans, you may end up delivering a different number. That is the result. It is a concrete figure, the consequence of the activity you have executed to reach the target. Results provide a clear indication of the quality of the planning, the ability to execute, upcoming risks and even the target's difficulty level. And while they mainly reflect the performance of the team, they can also be impacted by external events. If a regulatory rule modifies the price of a product unexpectedly, that would potentially generate a different result, moving closer to or further from the target.

Once you achieve the first set of results against the plan, you start the review process. Why did we deviate? Which assumptions did we get right or wrong? Which external conditions changed? Where did we do well or fail in execution? What unexpected issues did we face?

The next step is forecasting for the next period (month or quarter). Again, it is important to understand the details of the assumptions associated with the new prediction. From then onwards, you will handle the business reviews using three sets of numbers: targets, forecast and results. When you compare results against the last forecast, it is essential to understand what has happened. When you look at the new forecast, compare it with the target and build the plan to accomplish it.

In our business, as in many others, we presented our results quarterly. It triggered a lot of internal activity to check the performance from the last three months and throughout the fiscal year so far. The operational reviews, however, should be mainly structured to agree actions.

When I started, our reviews were just a few days after the previous quarter had closed, and they were mainly backward looking. They were focused on what had happened, the highlights and the lowlights of the previous period, the achievements, and the issues. Of course, we also discussed the future – the forecast, the actions, the risks and opportunities. But as the executive reviewer, you set the tone. I did not realise at the beginning that it permeates the whole organisation. If you structure the presentation, the financial focus, the content of the presentation to look backwards, you will end up with a whole organisation that is explaining the past. They will be collecting data and building presentations about what occurred, and focusing less on what the team is currently doing, and what they will need to succeed. The percentage of time you dedicate to each topic defines the priorities. More than you think.

We decided to change the reviews so that they took place in the middle of the quarter, instead of at the beginning. The presentation was more focused on the future. As it was closer to the end of the quarter, we had a better forecast and a clearer set of actions to execute. The conversation changed into the assumptions within that forecast, what help was needed, and how to deliver on every customer project that was critical for the results. We noticed a complete change across the whole business. In most meetings, agendas evolved to focus on what we were going to do, rather than checking what had happened and making a report about it. It applied to every aspect. People appraisals – a more balanced discussion about your performance against your development plan. Capex investments – aligning where you want to invest with future priorities.

The mindset continued to evolve from hope to confidence and determination.

I learned how the spirit of the whole organisation could be transformed with small, powerful signals. When you spend most of your time looking back, explaining the past, you have less control. If you change the focus, planning and discussing the future, and only use the past as a guide of lessons learned, you are in the driving seat. Your results will be the consequence of where you spend your time, effort and energy. My recommendation: rebalance the time you spend between reviewing the past (25%) and looking ahead (75%).

Create a can-do attitude

Performance reviews can be used to reinforce a can-do attitude. Most discussions will be around the content that your team bring to the meeting. However, you can also influence this to have a more productive discussion with a simple question: "What do you need?"

In a review of our Professional Services business, the team was presenting the evolution of the security services market. The rise in internet connectivity, and a growing e-commerce activity, had triggered an increase in cyber security risks. Companies' networks demanded more protection, which represented a unique opportunity for us. They were showing good growth in the business and solid plans to achieve it. However, they had awakened our excitement to aim for more. So, we launched our question: "Imagine you want to grow faster. What would you need?"

The team were well prepared. We started the discussion about increasing penetration in existing customers, finding new prospects, extending the portfolio and entering additional markets. For each of them, they explained the challenges, opportunities and resources they would need. Their job was to build the business case for each opportunity so that we could prioritise. Our job was to ask them what support they needed to execute and, once decided, provide it. We ended up approving some investments and recruiting more salespeople to accelerate growth. And the team delivered it.

This demonstrates the power of the question: What do you need? It will move people into a can-do attitude. They will focus on what they need to make something happen. Of course, there must be a clear contract between you and them. After asking, there should be a decision about who should find what is needed, and how.

Use paradoxical thinking to resolve conflicts

In business reviews, conflicting targets will appear. When this happens, you should be prepared to coach the team to use paradoxical thinking, because dealing with paradoxes is one of the biggest challenges of leadership. A paradox is when you face what appear to be contradictory statements. The question is how to make that paradox work. People who are used to linear thinking struggle with the ambiguity and out-of-the-box thinking to deal with paradoxes. And this happens everywhere.

Paradoxical thinking requires strong leadership. Consider, for example, the dilemma of improving service and reducing costs simultaneously. The first obvious reaction is that to provide better service, you might need more people. That increase would generate incremental costs and hence you are not able to deliver your second goal. I had this kind of discussion several times.

If you look at it in a linear way, this is true. You must improve how your services are implemented and you could indeed require additional resources. However, aiming to achieve both targets is when the paradoxical thinking is required.

In one of our management meetings, we were discussing how to take service to the next level. The direct answer from the Service Director was to recruit more project managers to increase the output by handling more orders. It would have generated incremental costs.

We did not have the budget to fund it. So, we agreed to look at more options. One of them was considering the amount of cost associated to failure. One reason why we needed to increase the costs was because some projects were late, and to deliver on time, you would need more people. Also, whenever mistakes were made, it would cost a lot to fix them. To resolve the paradox, we needed to focus on what we could do to reduce failure. Entering the data more accurately, setting more realistic delivery time frames, and double-checking work to avoid human error – these were all ways to reduce the cost base. And at the same time, the quality of service would improve immediately. Customers would be happier if solutions were delivered on time, and if service had no interruption.

Part of the cost saved could even be reinvested in more highly-skilled people, or in tools that could improve the service even further. So we built a plan to address the root causes of the cost of failure, and approved interim funding of temporary resources. The savings and additional revenues balanced the cost of the short-term actions within a few months.

I learned the power of paradoxical thinking to resolve apparently impossible contradictions.

Master information management

The Chief Execution Officer must be the master of understanding and managing the information of the company. In any organisation, you have enormous amounts of data. Classified data becomes information. Understanding information allows you to transform it into knowledge. That knowledge, filtered by experience, will evolve into wisdom.

In a mentoring session with a Spanish product manager, he asked: "Luis, I have read a lot of books about metrics, balance scorecards and how to monitor performance of businesses. How do you personally manage this? Given the amount of data you receive, how do you handle it? I guess that how you visualise and represent it could speed up your decision process. I am very interested to hear more about it."

He was right. The amount of data you get could be difficult to handle. You must define which are the key performance indicators you will follow, and identify the techniques you will use to look at information. This will allow you to make better decisions to support your vision. With a solid understanding of your business, areas of improvement will appear obvious.

Establish key business indicators

Identifying the business indicators will affect your ability to execute. You need metrics that provide you with guidance on how business is doing today, but also others that give you a view of the future. I like to separate lagging indicators from leading indicators.

Lagging indicators are output oriented. They are the results of your activity. For example, how much revenue you generate. They are the outcomes of your operations and they should be related to the vision you have defined. They are the targets for your business.

Leading indicators are input oriented. They create the results, hence you should focus on how to influence them. For example, the volume of contracts signed. They are the ones to impact because they are critical as they determine what will happen in the future. There is not always an easy correlation between lagging and leading indicators. However, you need both.

We were discussing which metrics to track, to make sure the business was progressing well. We defined the lagging indicators: revenue, EBITDA and cash. That was not difficult. However, we had myriads of leading indicators. Defining the architecture of KPIs is a critical task for the correct execution of your plans. It is like the control panel of a plane that allows you to steer the flight. We decided to look at four areas of activity to make it easier: growth, efficiency, service and people.

In growth, for example, we picked the number and value of orders signed as a leading indicator for revenue. In efficiency, we chose the cost of access lines from different suppliers. In service, a good indicator was the number of different types of incidents. Finally, for people we used, among other things, the biannual employee engagement survey. We created a Management Handbook, consolidating those KPIs and some more so that we could follow them easily. We also made sure that in different systems, like Salesforce, the metrics were clear, easy to track, and used often. I realised how important it is to define those metrics because what you follow, what you ask for, what you review is where the focus of the organisation will be.

Once key indicators are set, you must define how you are going to look at them. I found several ways in which you can organise data. Every person should decide which tools, graphics or reports to use. Make sure you spend time establishing yours. Everybody in the organisation must use them to run their part of the business, and they should become common tools and language. You must find the ones that are best for you. They will determine, to a large extent, how your organisation thinks.

Identify how you look at data

Consistency in using similar techniques has helped me to identify patterns and track performance, even across businesses that were quite different from one another. I used three easy but powerful techniques: quadrants, lists and waterfalls. Quadrants helped me to understand the business better by clustering. Lists enabled more focused execution by managing detailed plans. Waterfalls allowed good visibility of business dynamics, aiding the decision process.

Classify your data: Quadrants

Quadrants (2 x 2 tables) are one of my favourite classification tools. They can help you to discriminate any population of data and put the right focus on your key priorities. In its basic form, it is a 2-axis graph which you split into two halves. The result is four quadrants in which you position data based on a set of criteria. If you are immersed now in the world of big data, you would recognise its power. The objective is to split elements into clusters.

In big data techniques, learning can be implemented through supervised and unsupervised techniques. Supervised techniques use basic mathematical models like regression, to come to conclusions. Unsupervised learning is about clustering. It is about putting together elements that have common features. This is the way I used quadrants.

We were aiming to refine which customers should be our priority customers, so that we allocated our best resources to them. We completed a first analysis and found that the way we were managing our client base was not optimal. We decided to organise them based on two basic parameters: size and potential.

We placed current revenue in the horizontal axis, and potential for growth in the vertical axis. The higher you go, the greater the potential. The further to the right you go, the larger the revenue is. You can then classify your customers into four buckets. So, by mapping your customers on the quadrant, you will find four categories.

The bottom left quadrant will contain those customers with a small amount of business with you, and with low potential. You need to make sure you manage them using the most efficient channels, or find different ways to serve them, or even sell that part of your business to someone who can generate better value.

The top left quadrant will contain those customers whose business is small, but they have the potential to become larger customers. You need to be proactive with this segment. Take your 'hunters' and go after customers where the potential is significant. You must discriminate and be focused, as you cannot always pursue all the available opportunities. A strong development plan for each account will be a critical tool to understand where that potential really sits, and how to address it.

The bottom right quadrant will contain the customers where size is important, but they have low potential of generating incremental growth. This category normally includes long-term contracts with clear scope and almost no options to grow. For example, a government contract that had an open tender a few years ago, and once delivered, it is just about maintaining the level of profitability. In this space, you need strong contract management expertise and good risk management. Improving service will help to secure better levels of profitability when there are few alternatives to generate incremental business. High quality and low level of complaints means a happy customer, and no penalties that could damage the profitability.

The top right is where the core of your business should be. Those are the customers to focus on as a top priority, as they are your best opportunity for growth. Large business and large potential is any business leader's dream. Size means scale and, therefore, you can allocate your best resources here. Best quality people, combined with a high level of service, means a more satisfied customer – and converting the potential into real business should be easier to achieve.

CUSTOMER SEGMENTATION

+		
POTENTIAL	Focus to win	Invest to grow
	Manage efficiently	Serve to maximise return
–		
	– **SIZE** **+**	

We learned so much about the business that we grew twice as fast across the customers we prioritised. We stopped wasting time and effort on those that were less valuable for our business. This is how we used quadrants for clustering.

Simplify by managing by lists

To some extent, most of the complexity of a business can be summarised in simple parameters. We are all used to working with lists, at the supermarket or when you prepare the list of invitees to a party. It is a simple way of managing things. This is why I used lists as a simple way to run some of our operations.

I had a discussion with our CIO at the time about how to instil in our teams the passion to know the details. We were wondering how to create it with a simple way of managing information. In the end we agreed that, in a business-to-business operation, you can pretty much run your business through the right set of lists. I know this may sound simplistic but it is really effective.

First, you should have a list of your customers, and for each customer you should have a list of their attributes – how many connections or products they have. You should go deep into this so that you fully understand each customer. A forensic perspective will give you the status of each line or service and then allow you to take action against each.

When you run a project to connect a customer's premises and factories, again you should have a list, whether it is 10 sites or 500 sites. A good project manager will be able to go through it and define priorities, identify risks and show progress – just by dealing with the list. To some extent, it is a form of testing how well an organisation can break a very large and complex problem into smaller pieces or units. Of course, managing that list is more complex than writing it on paper or even in a simple Excel spreadsheet – it relies on having the right systems. However, the concept remains valid, and it makes complex problems simpler: define which lists you can use to manage them. I have learned that if you don't know which lists you need to run any piece of business, you might need to rethink how you are controlling it.

Use waterfalls to describe the hydraulics of the business

A challenge for your Execution dimension is to discover the dynamics of the business you run. I found waterfalls to be a useful tool when it comes to dissecting the operational and financial KPIs.

In one of our planning cycles, we were trying to understand how we could achieve the revenue of the next fiscal year. We wanted to work out what the key areas of focus were and, based on the revenue of the current fiscal period, consider potential changes. Breaking the revenue into pieces would make it easier to make decisions and have a clear view of what can be achieved. So we built a waterfall.

To do this, you should take the amount of business generated the previous year and break it up into pieces. The first piece is the specific items that were unique last year, the one-offs. Things that happened only once, that won't be repeated in the same form – such as selling equipment to a customer who was setting up a new network. The next piece to consider is the business you have lost: churn. For example, the cancellation of a customer contract with recurrent revenue. A third element would be caused by price reduction, either contractually committed or because of new negotiations. These three deductions, when taken out of your existing revenue, will leave you with the underlying income of your business.

Now you need to start adding up new revenue opportunities. The first is the same kind of one-offs you can win next year. A second one would be associated to the deals you have already signed, which are in delivery and will be ready to generate incremental revenue. A third one would be produced by business that has still to be won, either identified or even unknown yet.

Splitting your data into separate elements helps to understand the business, the risks and the opportunities, and how challenging a budget or plan really is.

How was I using it? Well, when looking to the previous period's one-offs, the key questions are about repeatability and focus, margins and incentives for salespeople.

The cancellations, or churn, force a debate around the reasons for losing, regretted losses and how to keep the business and the margins for as long as possible. For example, reducing the resources allocated to a contract that has been lost, while delivering against commitments, and charging for every cost incurred, as contractually agreed.

On price reductions, the main question is around the specifics. When do they take effect? Which elements are they applicable to?

I knew a Sales Director in Belgium who had a great way of coaching his team on this. A customer was asking for a 10% price reduction. We could not say no to a reduction; if we did, they would have gone to open tender, which would have been more expensive for us. The Account Manager was trying to reduce the size of the reduction by explaining the value of our services. In the first internal discussion, the team were debating whether to give 5% or the 10% that the customer was asking for. The Sales Director asked why the decision was between 5% or 10%. He suggested offering 6.54%. When you go down to two decimal places, you have a larger range for negotiation. In any case, the way you run your business requires that level of detail. It is important to save as much profit as you can. I realise how important it is to create this mindset that every penny counts.

When it comes to adding incremental business to your waterfall, your questions should be focused on the trends. What is the historical trend in one-offs? Do you have a similar volume every year? Have you already identified those opportunities?

Revenue generated by projects you have already won is a key business driver. What are the assumptions or dependencies? When will delivery begin? What are the risks?

And finally, the unknown sources of revenue: projects to be won, or even new opportunities to be found. What is the win rate? What is the size of the pipeline of deals already identified? When you apply those ratios, how much new business do you still need to find?

If you put all this into an equation:

New year's revenue = Last year's revenue – One-offs – Churn – Price reductions + One-offs + Delivery of won projects + Business to win

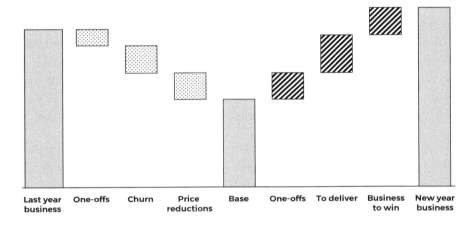

| Last year business | One-offs | Churn | Price reductions | Base | One-offs | To deliver | Business to win | New year business |

You can easily follow the hydraulics of your business. We applied them also to margins, cash and other key parameters.

What I learned about waterfalls is that they are also one of the best tools for business performance reviews. You can cascade the same approach to lower levels of the organisation. We used it extensively. They forced people to have a superior understanding of the dynamics of their businesses.

Evaluate individual performance

Once you have defined expectations and set targets, established the method to track performance and decided how you manage business information, it is time to evaluate individual performance.

The basis of personal performance evaluation is discussing the areas in which someone has done well and the areas that require improvement. You should have this discussion from different perspectives. First, you should have a good balance between on-the-moment feedback and formal interventions. Second, you should create an environment for bold improvements in what people do, and how they do it. Third, you should use benchmarking as a way of providing a best-in-class perspective to the discussion.

Create formal and informal feedback moments

As part of the coaching role we discussed earlier, assessing results is essential to driving high performance. High performance is well understood when linked to sports. In most disciplines, your first competitor is yourself. Your ambition to improve, and always do better – for example, making incremental gains to run a millisecond faster, or improve your jump to score more points in basketball. But you also compete with others. If you are a world record runner, your competitors are the fastest on the globe.

All top athletes use coaches or trainers who will advise on their strengths and weaknesses, and where they need to improve. They provide feedback in the moment, during the game, but also in training moments or reviewing videos of matches. It is the same in business. You should give your team instant feedback when you think it is needed and, at the same time, make sure you prepare well for the quarterly or annual appraisals.

In one of our leadership team meetings, a young project manager came to present a new network solution for which we had been waiting for some time. One of my direct reports asked a few aggressive questions about the delay and made comments about the competence of the people leading the launch. The project manager clearly felt uncomfortable and we brought the conversation back into a positive zone. At the end of the meeting, I called my colleague into my office. I asked him what he thought of his actions. He believed it was unacceptable to have such a delay, although he recognised he should have reacted differently. He apologised to the presenter and took it into account for the future. On-the-moment feedback is a great informal way of making people think.

Those flashes of instant feedback should mean that there are no surprises when it comes to the annual appraisal. Make sure you don't keep all your comments back for the formal discussions. Those examples permit a fruitful conversation. Evaluating personal performance is a key task of the CEO. High-ranking executives also deserve proper feedback and a detailed discussion. Very few people are prepared to tell them what they do well and what they should develop or change. I used to spend around an hour preparing each individual review, looking not just at what they had delivered but also how they did it. How they displayed the values of the company and worked with the rest of the team.

If your organisation asks you to provide ratings as part of the process, make sure you focus the discussion on the essentials and not the rating itself. The most important part of those appraisals is the conversation.

When talking about business, I found that three categories could facilitate a focused debate. How the individual has been and will be:

- Running the business. This is about making sure the responsibilities and core functions of the job are going well, delivering operational excellence. This could include improvements in service, cost or people management.

- Growing the business. In every unit, there is a growth opportunity. Sales can win more business; service can improve what they do and charge for the improved quality. This is about creating incremental value for the company.

- Changing the business. In a world of constant change, identifying areas for transformation and executing them properly makes a difference. A solid executive should be a change engine for the organisation.

I like separating the three aspects during those assessments. You provide your examples, but allow the person's views to enrich the discussion. Then you also add the values of the company to the conversation. This is a great example of the combination of the Engagement and Execution dimensions.

Be bold on improvements

To drive high performance, each period must be better than the last – for everybody. The bar of excellence rises every year. Customers become more demanding, competitors get cleverer, technology offers new opportunities, and people become increasingly effective and highly skilled. So, what was good last year is no longer enough today. This is crucial for performance discussions. You must be bold when it comes to asking for improvements. It must be well explained and understood. It might sound easy, however it is not.

In a performance review with a sales director a few years ago, we were looking at the actual performance and the challenges to keep doing better. He said: "I have been working very hard." But when we reviewed the results, they were not what we had agreed. Hard work is important but it is not everything. He felt that the targets were becoming more and more difficult. "It is true, our customers are more challenging," I said. "We must respond by working in a smarter way and being more effective. It is not about spending more hours in the office. It is the opposite: it is about optimising the use of your working time. You can ask for help. But you should be realistic. This is going to continue forever. We should get better every year to maintain our ability to compete and serve our customers. Think about how you want to face this challenge." After a few days, he came back and we discussed his targets and what he would need to do to achieve them.

Replicate success

I have seen in some organisations that great performance is made visible. There are many ways of showing it to the rest of the organisation. You can nominate an 'employee of the month' and put a picture on the wall. You can put some balloons on the desk of the best agent in a call centre, as I saw in a US airline a few years ago. In India, it worked well to have the graphs with individual and team results published on a board.

But the most important thing is to foster peer-to-peer recognition as a team habit. We used to publish our monthly role models. This public recognition encouraged others to learn from them.

One of my favourite books describes this important effect: *Contagious Success* by Susan Lucia Anunzio. It reflects on how you can create a high-performance organisation by driving a certain mindset – a mentality of replicating success by looking at your best performers.

We had a review with a voice product manager. He had been doing a good job since he started as a graduate, with the ambition to do better every year. However, he was also focused on the quality of his work and he wanted to get the highest rating – 5 out of 5 – in his annual performance review. His boss and I liked his energy and determination. He also knew that he had great potential but also a lot to learn. The voice industry was moving fast, becoming digital. A challenging market always brings opportunities to learn.

During the review, his boss, who was well prepared for these conversations, focused on the good things that he had developed: flexible price propositions, solid margin improvement plans, and fresh customer tools to make self-provisioning easier. He was proud. Then, his boss reflected on the areas he needed to improve: more customer focus, faster go-to-market and more innovation. He gave him a 4 out of 5. He was visibly disappointed. He asked why he did not get the 5. His boss said: "You have done a good job. You have delivered well what was expected of you. And you have great talent to grow. However, there are things you can do much better." So, we recommended he should learn from other people, from the best. I asked him to think about four questions:

- Who is best in class in your kind of job in your department?

- Who is best in class in your kind of job in your company?

- Who is best in class in the market?

- What are the attributes, level of knowledge, attitude and experience of the best in any of these three levels?

By asking those questions you will be open to compare and learn. This kind of benchmarking applies to the Execution dimension of the CEO. You should consider who is best in the industry, or across industries, and why. It will complement your self-awareness. I learned a lot by doing this.

Connect the dots

Performance is not even across your business. Some units will execute their plans better than others, achieving better results. Even with similar activities, there will be teams that will be able to excel beyond expectations. In most organisations, I found it difficult to share that ability to execute across the company. In some instances, it is down to individuals; in others, it is the way the team works together, or even the way a team makes use of a company tool, smarter than other teams. The CEO has a privileged position, being able to see these buckets of brilliance and helping to spread them across the business. You get to participate in dozens of conversations and meetings across the globe, and lots of projects, ideas and initiatives pass by your desk. By observing everything, you can suggest which elements could be applied to other areas of the business to improve their efficiency. You can identify duplication that can be eliminated. I call this 'connecting the dots'. Fostering sharing as a way of improving. Stimulating cross-fertilisation and encouraging people to work together.

Encourage sharing

The Chief Execution Officer is the main witness of great performance. So, he can act as the facilitator of collaboration. In a large, dispersed organisation, great ideas could easily get lost. The CEO, and the whole leadership team, should not underestimate their personal role when it comes to pushing the company to share. Sharing is an attitude, a mindset. Whenever you find something you like, you should ask: "Who have you shared this with?"

As the CEO, you must proactively drive sharing. You can easily connect the dots.

I met with a finance team in Spain that had a powerful tool to calculate the margins of products and services. It meant they could understand their profitability better, making smarter offers and planning more effective sales incentives. I remembered that managing product margins was a challenge in some parts of our Latin American business, so I asked the Spanish team to contact them and see what could be shared. It turned out that they could reuse most of the system and quickly improve their margins.

Sharing is one of the most powerful tools to improve business. You must encourage it but it cannot be dependent on you. As a great advocate of it, you can lead by example and celebrate when it happens. Ask your team to build tools and methods that will facilitate sharing, such as an application or a forum where ideas can be discussed. The best outcome would be for people to share openly because they want others to do well.

Stimulate cross-fertilisation

Sharing is one way of leveraging your ability to connect the dots. It gives others access to things that have worked well elsewhere. You can take this one step further. People can start co-creating and building on others' ideas. You would end up with an enhanced solution for the whole company.

The Professional Services team was made up of 3,000 people across 12 countries. They had been operating in an isolated manner for some time. We wanted to make them a truly global team while also making sure they were focused on local business. In one of our meetings in Singapore, we found a successful customer proposition, providing advice to companies that wanted to move to Cloud services. While we had similar ideas in France and Brazil, no one else had put together this quality of proposition. So, we put together a team with representatives from Singapore, France and Brazil, and challenged them to build something reusable. They took the Asian proposition as the foundation and cross-fertilised it with experiences and ideas from the others. They ended up with a stronger solution, easier to sell and with a high value for customers. We called it 'Quick Start'.

We decided to apply the same methodology to the disperse propositions which had been built in several places. The joint effort of the teams to build something global was fantastic. At the end of the process, we had more than 40 of these Quick Start propositions. We used a tool called 'Wizard' to set up an open community where you could ask a question to your Professional Services colleagues around the globe – for instance: "Has anyone done a contact centre project using Microsoft technologies?" More importantly, there was a new way of working together.

This cross-fertilisation between teams can happen with products, with the way offers are built, or the way you build services for customers. However, you need to be personally committed to it. In large organisations, it is easy to focus on your own area of business or country if you don't make the time or the contacts to learn or share about what others do.

We decided to foster collaboration across countries by launching an international rotation programme. We picked around 40 people – 'talent' – from different countries and offered them a three-month project in a different place. After a careful selection process, they worked in their hosting destinations. I attended the closing event of the first cohort and it was fascinating. They had learned so much about the host business unit and compared it with their home one. They had developed a great network that they would use for years to come, and they brought new ideas to both of their units. I found it inspiring and a great way of breaking boundaries.

Use curiosity to drive collaboration

Connecting the dots requires a good understanding of the business. To have this, you must be actively curious.

I was in Gurgaon, India, visiting our service operation centre. I met one of the teams serving a large global company. They had achieved the best score in customer loyalty and satisfaction, and I was curious about it. So I asked: "How did you get such a good score?" They have a very satisfied customer with a good working relationship. Why? They have consistently delivered on time and provided them with accurate billing. How? They have good information and a robust process. What's that? They built a simple tool with all the delivery data and the billing information.

We looked at the tool. It was very good and simple to apply to other customers. So, we started implementing it with several other teams and we quickly felt the benefits in customer perception. It showed me the importance of getting a deeper understanding and then looking for opportunities to connect the dots.

Reflection

Driving high performance is a key activity for the Chief Execution Officer. Being demanding is an essential part of flawless execution. Some basics are essential to make it happen:

- How do you make your expectations clear to your team or even to your colleagues?
- How do you set targets that are well defined and aligned to your vision?
- How do you track performance? Looking backwards or forwards?
- When was last time you defined your key metrics?
- Which tools and techniques do you use to track them? Why?
- When you evaluate performance, how well do you prepare?
- Which examples do you have of connecting the dots?

CHAPTER VIII

STAY FOCUSED ON EXECUTING THE VISION

The Chief Execution Officer is responsible for keeping the focus on what matters. This means pushing for the critical activities that will make the vision happen and forgetting other paths. It is easy to get distracted – unexpected calls, incidents, unplanned meetings, urgent emails or market changes. The discipline of staying focused will be essential to secure a successful execution.

To stay focused, you should prioritise, simplify, keep calm, delegate and be ready to partner.

Prioritise

Time, as I already mentioned, is your most scarce resource. Deciding where to spend your time is your most important decision. We live in an always-on world. We receive news every second, through multiple channels, and we are often requested to respond. Deciding what to do first and what to leave for later is a challenge. I have found myself, on several occasions, driven by my calendar and not by my decisions on what was a priority. So, I decided to do three things:

- Constantly refer to my initial plan to check and review priorities

- Differentiate between what is urgent and what is important

- Learn to say no

Plan your first days

Of course, to be able to refer to your initial plan, you need a plan. You might have read *The First 90 Days* by Michael Watkins. I have used this text several times in my career. I like it because it can be applied to any job, whether it is new or you just need a fresh perspective.

You must create your own personal plan and stick to it. You might need to adjust or modify it but make sure you have it as your personal guide. It can be for your 90 days or 100 days – it does not matter as long as it contains those 'must do' activities. Put as much detail into it as possible. Make it personal. It should be your plan, not the plan for the company or for your team.

When I was appointed as CEO, I built a 90-day plan. It included items where I had to act, and where I decided to focus my attention:

- The team. It was key to know them, their ambitions and their plans; assess their capabilities and whether we were ready to work together. I had to know quickly the changes I had to make. I planned long, individual meetings.

- The customers. I needed to know who the main customers were, the main opportunities to be won and the main issues to be addressed.

I decide to call them personally, and organised calls and meetings to review them.

- The financials. I had to understand how solid the plans were, the main risks to be tackled and the time frame. I had to decide how to balance short-term targets with long-term sustainable performance.

I also reviewed several areas like portfolio and service. I visited countries and teams from different units. I engaged with the board and other external stakeholders such as investors, journalists and analysts. As part of the first 90-day plan, we established the articulation of the vision as a priority.

I used this plan as a key reference. It was worth spending time on it.

Separate what is urgent from what is important

A strong plan should be your guide to execution. However, when you are appointed, your inbox will be full of congratulations, welcome messages, ideas and urgent requests. Those could be great opportunities to take the pulse of the organisation as long as you stay focused. It took me some time to differentiate between what was important and what was urgent.

I received an email from a marketing leader with the subject 'Urgent decision'. As I was new in the job, I didn't want to miss any big issues, so I started to read it. There was a 20-page PowerPoint presentation attached. When I went through it, I realised that it was indeed urgent: we had to approve the launch of a product so that it could be developed in time to meet the agreed date. However, it was urgent for the person who had to deliver it. I had no clue whether it was critical for the company or not. And in fact, when I went deeper, it wasn't. The urgency was for him, not for me. With an email subject like that, he just wanted to capture my attention – and it worked. I learned that urgency is subjective and you should teach your team to use it properly, otherwise you will only pay attention to those who shout the loudest.

If something is urgent, you should decide and then execute quickly. If something is important, you should spend quality time analysing and resolving it accordingly.

Learn to say no

Making decisions and implementing them is the way you will make an impact. To maintain the focus on the critical ones, you should develop a rare skill: learning to say no. Saying no is easy. Saying no to the right things is more difficult. An organisation that can say no in a clever manner is stronger. It reduces the time wasted on the wrong activities or discussions. Your team should feel empowered to do it.

I met our team in Dubai and we were discussing how to be more efficient. They complained about the number of reports they had to prepare. In most cases, the requests came with a message: 'Luis has asked for this report'. I like using information and data as a way to understand the business and make better decisions, but I have always tried to use reports that already exist, to avoid wasting people's time. So I told them that they could say no if they thought the request was nonsense, and it was not explained to them why it was needed. In fact, I committed to only asking for information or reports that people would need to do their job properly.

Saying no to suppliers also helps the relationship. I had a discussion with the head of a software company who was trying to sell his product. They wanted to run a pilot with us, but it was not a priority for us. Our team was trying to be polite, but this was delaying the discussion. So, when we clearly said that we were not going to do it, we could move on. We stopped wasting time on both sides and started looking at other opportunities to collaborate.

Saying no quickly is fundamental to staying focused.

Simplify

Simplification is a natural focus for any new CEO. Organisations tend to get complicated over time. Departments are created to support projects or ideas, and at the end of the project we forget to close the department. Duplicated initiatives appear around new technologies. The integration of acquisitions is not always as smart as initially intended. The result is a degree of entropy. It causes additional cost, not just in resources but also in the amount of effort to overcome the bureaucracy it generates. When companies go through crisis periods there is a strong focus on reducing costs. Simplification is a good method. However, there is always the risk that 'controlling units' pop up everywhere, to keep control of the simplification.

To drive a robust simplification initiative, you must remove all unnecessary efforts happening in the organisation, you should build trust, and you drive a simpler structure of the operating and support units.

Remove unnecessary work

I like Amazon's approach to 'act as a day 1 company'. One of their ambitions is to avoid most of the burden of a large and complex enterprise. Companies that have built structures over many years can end up with several layers of organisation, and accidentally keep units that support a previous strategy that is no longer relevant. Keeping up the discipline of consistently cleaning a business is hard. Therefore, there is always an opportunity for a newcomer to do it, and it can be done regardless of whether you have risen through the ranks or come from outside the company.

This reminds me of one of my first conversations with Claire Williams and her team. Claire is the daughter of Frank Williams, the brilliant Formula One driver and founder of the Williams F1 racing team and all their associated activities. They were driving a major transformation in the way they build cars, from design to execution. New talent was a key part of it and they brought in Graeme Hackland as the CIO. I always felt inspired listening to him. One of the best stories they told was about focus. Keeping the focus on everything and not getting distracted. They decided to 'stop any activity that was not focused on making the car go faster'. I loved it.

I wondered how many times we do things without a clear purpose. I kept questioning: Were we rigorous enough in stopping things that were not 'making our car go faster'? This applies in every business, regardless of what 'the car' is and whichever performance metric needs to 'go faster'. I found myself answering this question and concluding that we still had duplication, and we were still spending time and effort on unnecessary activity. It is a good concept at any level of any company.

Build trust

In some cases, complexity is linked to the creation of too many control units, whose main purpose is 'checking the checkers'. When companies go through difficult moments, they protect themselves by creating these departments. There are two risks with this. First, it creates additional complexity and cost, which could slow down the whole organisation if the power of those units grows too much. Second, it creates a lack of real accountability, as some people could rely on the control units for it.

A great way of simplifying is allocating strong accountability to the operational leaders, trusting them, building clear controls and applying consequence management accordingly.

After acquiring a company, we found that they had a strong supervisory structure. They were reviewing and controlling every single order signed by their sales teams. Their aim was to make sure that the valuation was correct. The sales teams had their own unit doing this as well, to make sure that when challenged by the control unit, they could show their own calculations. It was a clear example of lack of trust and, as a result, duplication. We changed the process so that only a few samples would get reviewed, and we put in place strong consequence management for anyone who got their information wrong. We made it clear that the accountability for providing accurate data was with the sales team. We saved time, money and effort, we secured good governance, and we empowered our people to do their jobs properly.

Trust is a powerful instrument for driving agility in business. It can be easily supported with the right level of controls, which should be independent, rigorous and parallel to the business. Good governance with several lines of defence, strong internal and external audit teams and visible leadership can be simple as well. I found that you, in your Execution dimension, must demonstrate the non-negotiable aspect of solid governance. Your behaviour will inspire the behaviour of others.

Make a simpler organisation

Complexity develops with the growth, expansion and globalisation of businesses. New roles are created without making sure they are clearly distinct from existing ones. Job descriptions don't always define scopes well enough. This happens even more when new functions or technologies appear. In this scenario, it is easy to create additional management layers within those new functions. There must be a custodian of the organisational model who restricts the uncontrolled appearance of jobs or functions that do not serve the model.

When I started as CEO, we reviewed all the jobs and functions across the business. We created a kind of 'war room' where we pinned up all the top-level organisation charts from across the business. By visualising it, we gained a better perspective of the organisation. We closed units that were doing duplicate jobs. We discovered several jobs that weren't defined clearly enough, and consolidated multiple functions into one. By bringing together teams that were in small, disperse locations, we improved processes and became more agile. It took us six months to execute the plan. I realised how important it is to keep questioning how simple your configuration is, and whether every single job should exist.

Keep calm

As CEO, you will always come up against issues and challenges. Your ability to deal with them will be determined by the way you react. Panic is your worst enemy. Resilience is the core skill you will need to develop. I like Rudyard Kipling's poem *If*. In particular, the lines: *If you can keep your head when all about you are losing theirs…* and *If you can meet with Triumph and Disaster and treat those two impostors just the same…* I used it as inspiration for many years.

I have met failure in many moments in my life. Those were situations in which I also learned a lot. My main advice is to keep calm and focus on action. First assess the impact and then react fast to the most affected areas with clear plans. Afterwards, work on the root causes, which takes more time. Finally, create a learning culture, not a blaming one.

Assess the impact

Your problems can range from technical failures and regulatory changes to a cybersecurity attack and unexpected internal challenges. It is very important to assess the impact before making an uncontrolled reaction. This will allow you to better understand what is happening, so that you can act fast. The speed of response should include a communication strategy. If there are customer or market implications, you need a plan on how to explain what has happened, and the actions you have taken. We have witnessed CEOs communicating too early, without proper information, which puts their credibility at risk. Just keep calm.

Many years ago, we built a market plan to launch a mobile virtual network operator. The business plan was solid. It included the existing regulatory framework as an assumption. Three months after it was launched, the regulatory authority decided to change interconnection charges. It put the whole business case at risk. We reconsidered the offering we were making. Margins were heavily affected, and we were obliged to reduce the ambitions of the plan. Our risk register was not good enough and we were not well enough prepared. However, it was important to look at the impact and minimise the damage in the short term, whilst getting ready for a new longer-term strategy. We experienced some tense moments, but keeping calm was important.

The most difficult issues are those that generate a big impact on the service to customers, whether it is an interruption to a large population of consumers or a complete outage in only one customer. In both cases, resolution is the priority. Your role in this case is to allow the team to work on the issue, arranging emergency conference calls to keep them coordinated.

In a financial services entity, we had scheduled a change to install a new security certificate. Everything looked fine on the Sunday night, but the following morning some electronic banking services were not working. We got the alert and the team was mobilised to look at the details. After a few hours, the glitch was found and sorted. I kept direct contact with the customer's executives and made sure that resources were available to the team sorting the issue. I remembered from my time as an engineer that the

CEO, in those moments, could only do one useful thing: bring pizza to the engineers working on the incident.

Address root causes

Keeping calm in the first instance should be complemented with a strong practice to find the root causes of the issues. Understanding systematically the reasons behind problems should become part of the DNA of any company.

We established weekly service meetings to tackle those problems. We used three questions consistently:

- Do we know the root cause of the problem? Sometimes you could get distracted by the symptoms, without going any further. Like in health, high temperature or cough are just symptoms, and it is better to go after the root cause of the illness.

- Do we have a plan to address it? Understanding root causes is key, but you should build a well-defined plan to resolve them. A plan must have activities, owners and timescales.

- Are we executing the plan? Having a plan is not enough if you have not allocated the required resources, systems or tools to execute it.

Doing this systematically created a culture of understanding and focus on execution. It helped everybody prepare to answer them.

Develop a learning culture, not a blaming one

In all those difficult moments, there is one temptation: finding out who is to blame. The CEO can create a cultural shift away from this. It is important to know where responsibility lies, and to hold people accountable. However, the focus should be on the lessons learned. You set the tone from the top. Spending time pointing to members of the team is a waste of time. It could even encourage people to hide behind excuses or put the blame on external elements. The more you can register the lessons learned, and how to spread the learning across the business, the better.

At the beginning of my career, I worked with a leader who, most of the time, was focused on finding out who was guilty. It created an environment of fear and lack of trust. Nobody wanted to take any responsibility and he ended up being the sole accountable person of the whole organisation. It was a vicious circle. When new issues appeared, he needed more people to blame. Anxiety also made individuals fail more frequently, as they were less confident. We learned nothing, as root causes were never actually identified and addressed. Failure became a personal drama instead of a source of corporate experience and incremental knowledge. I learned at that time how not to deal with failure.

More recently, I worked with leaders focusing on understanding why things happened. Of course, people were held accountable and tough actions were taken. However, the focus was on preventing it from happening again elsewhere. Frustration and disappointment were shared openly, with a clear message of looking ahead. We put plans into action to avoid it happening again. I learned the relevance of balancing toughness with determination to learn to prevent future issues.

Delegate

You will not have the time to deal with everything that happens in your company. So, you must delegate responsibilities and decisions to your team. This is the management side of the empowered team we discussed before. It will provide you with the management bandwidth needed to focus on your own responsibilities and decisions, those that only you can uniquely own. You must decide which ones to deputise. A great way of allocating decisions is to put as many as you can closer to the customer. You can also create mini-CEOs, as I will describe later, who can acquire leadership skills by having greater accountability. It will mean, however, that you and the whole team must master risk management when cascading delegation authority.

Bring decisions close to the customer

Your span of management is smaller than you think. You may feel that your knowledge and experience qualifies you to make better decisions than those who are in direct contact with customers or local businesses.

Unfortunately, that is not true, and if it is true, you have the wrong team. For sure, you could easily waste your time approving vacancies for new jobs or questioning a discount for a customer. But you should stay focused on the big picture.

We had put in place a set of rigorous controls around hiring new people, to prevent unnecessary recruitment. So, if someone wanted to recruit for a role, they had to submit the business case to a central filtering team, regardless of where they were in the world. This team would decide if the role was justified enough. After a few months, we realised the central team didn't have enough context to make the decisions. So, for every job they should come back to the requesting unit to discuss and understand it better.

I remember one discussion about a sales role in Argentina. After three weeks of going backwards and forwards, we put the decision back with the country manager. They knew their business environment better than anyone centrally. We decided that it was better to allow each unit to judge the resources they needed. We would hold them accountable for the result of their business targets.

I have heard similar discussions about whether or not call centre agents should be able to provide special offers or pay rebates. Deciding where to put the threshold of decision-making responsibility is important. But we learned that you save more money by placing the responsibility in the field, rather than having a complicated approval process. Customer satisfaction also grew because of the change in policy for the front-end delegation.

Create mini-CEOs

Delegating authority does not only save you time, it also helps the team to understand what it means to be a CEO. You can identify areas of expertise that you want your team to master, and put them down to their direct responsibility.

An example of larger delegation is sales leadership: responsibility for making offers and managing margins, supplier negotiations, recruitment, managing resources, restructuring teams, launching services and marketing campaigns. Real or virtual profit and loss accounts (P&Ls) can be used to evaluate the quality of decisions. Training on the job will be more powerful than any course. You will improve the way they respond to challenges.

We created large account management positions as a 'mini-CEO' job. They owned the P&L and the relationship with the customer. They had to find new opportunities to grow the business, improve the efficiency and cost base to deliver high profits, secure adequate levels of resources, set risk registers, and establish strong governance in their contracts. Some of them struggled with such a broad range of responsibilities. However, it was a fantastic education for those who really wanted to become a CEO in the future. It gave us visibility of the future leaders of the business. We could test their capabilities in a ring-fenced environment. Some of them succeeded and progressed up the ladder. I learned about the power of delegating and empowering.

Master risk management

Delegating is also an opportunity to reinforce a critical capability in today's businesses: risk management. Managing risk as part of decision-making processes can be a differentiator. Organisations that do well at assessing the risks are more informed when it comes to making decisions. You should start by identifying the risks and compiling them in a risk register. You should consider the likelihood of an event happening and its potential impact. You could even categorise the list within a 2x2 quadrant and then decide the priorities.

Once you have each individual risk, you can define the appetite to take that risk, and the mitigating actions you need to take to minimise it.

When we pushed for larger delegation of authority in some units, we also launched a disciplined campaign to create and manage risk registers across the business. We considered risk management to be a critical tool for improving the running of the business. However, it took some time to embed it completely across the organisation. For example, when we asked for the risk register in a contract review, the list only contained two items. The list was so short because the team did not think the rest were worth mentioning. However, the potential impact of some of these 'smaller' risks was huge. They considered the likelihood to be small, so they had not taken any mitigating actions to cover such significant regulatory risk. Good practice would have been to register it and be prepared. After a few months, it became normal practice to discuss the individual risks in management meetings or contracts reviews.

You, as the leader, must set the tone from the top. Just by asking about the risks, and discussing the mitigating plans, the whole organisation will realise its importance.

Learn to partner

Staying focused also means establishing the core of what you do – and what you don't do. It does not mean that you cannot provide certain services to your customers; instead, you decide what you will do yourself, and what you will provide with the use of partners. In this way, you will focus on what you are best at. And you will begin to see and treat your 'suppliers' as true 'partners'. Partnering is increasingly an ecosystem play. Companies are choosing more and more to share developments and launch products together. Leading the ecosystem can be a business opportunity, leveraging the vast majority of the industry to create value for your organisation.

Establish your core

When you look at any business activity, there are three strategies you can follow: build, buy or partner.

You can build a new information system or a new product. The decision to do it in-house is normally based on how close it is to the core business of the company. Developing a capability normally takes time and it should be associated with the value creation you are looking for.

Buying offers you the possibility of acquiring a competence faster. But it can have a higher short-term cost, so you must make a strategic decision about the element you want to add and how close it is to the core business. Then it is just a question of making a business case to see if it is better to build or buy.

Those two strategies will enhance and develop your core. You should spend time defining that core. It should be linked to your vision and it should be your focus.

Partnering is slightly different. It should be used when the capabilities are needed for your business to succeed, but they are not core to your vision. It would be complementary, and in many cases essential, to your fundamental propositions. Therefore, clever partnering is a key consideration in your Execution dimension.

Our Cloud of Clouds portfolio vision was gaining traction in the market. A good number of analysts and customers were excited about the inspiring opportunity that our proposition was bringing to them. But we needed the full support of another key set of stakeholders: our partners.

In an industry that evolves so fast, partnership required intimacy, knowledge and open collaboration. We partnered with well-known global players, such as Cisco for critical network equipment, EMC for their increased capabilities in the Cloud, and Nokia for their virtualised network solutions. Our role was to keep learning about their areas of investment, and how we could work with them to provide solutions that customers were demanding. We mapped all their products and services, defined the areas we wanted to build ourselves, and decided where we needed to partner to complete our vision. It saved time and allowed us to remain focused.

Build partnerships, not supplier relationships

A supplier is someone from whom you buy a product under a set of terms and conditions. You will need suppliers for a significant part of your operations. A solid procurement process will allow you to optimise the way you operate with them. But in some cases, you might need a stronger relationship with, and the involvement of, the companies you work with.

This might be because you want to know in advance what new features they will add to their products. You might even be able to influence which characteristics should be part of their portfolio roadmap. Or perhaps you want to co-create some solutions with co-investments. You will need to disclose your own plans to make sure that collaboration is successful. You could share resources, seconding people temporarily to the other company. This is partnership and it is critical in complex and rapidly evolving markets.

Working with partners, I learned to consider a few things:

- Why should I partner? Identify the partner's area of expertise that brings value to your business or your customers.

- Where are they investing? This should reassure you that their investments are in line with your vision, and that they are committed to your vision.

- How will you engage with them? Define which products, resources or investments are involved in the partnership agreement.

- And finally, why do they want to partner with you? This will give you an idea of the strength of the partnership.

We were discussing the evolution of our portfolio. We wanted to develop computer processing power and storage in the Cloud. Leading players had already been investing in and developing solid propositions in their web services. We analysed whether or not it made sense for us to compete with them. The answer was no. The amount of money they had invested, and the scale they were reaching, were far from our core ambitions. So, we decided to establish a partnership model. We looked at the capabilities our customers were demanding and how we could respond with the new relationships. We established an operating framework to integrate our services with leading Cloud providers. For them, it was a solid go-to-market proposition for large businesses; for us, we ended up with a richer offering that made a difference for our customers.

Leverage the ecosystem

The Chief Execution Officer can use partnership to create new operating models. In most industries, there is a great interrelation between companies that are working in different fields. Some are competitors and others collaborate. The financial services industry is a great example. There is a new set of startups using technology to develop financial services propositions, called Fintechs. Someone could leverage the power of those players by creating a marketplace where they can offer their products. If it were a trusted environment, it would attract the customers and partners of those Fintechs, making the ecosystem more significant. The larger the number of members, the higher the value you would create.

We had a leading financial services network in the Cloud. It managed to create a partnership model that was quite unique in the industry. Over 2,000 applications and several thousands of partners operated in a secure environment. New companies could bring their solutions to the marketplace. Offering an open platform made it easy to incorporate new services and to consume them. It would have been impossible for any company to build such a broad set of solutions from scratch. However, the power of the ecosystem made it possible, even for competing companies. I learned that by staying focused you could create, develop and use partnerships to strengthen your core business.

Reflection

In this chapter, we have discussed the importance of staying focused to maximise your Execution dimension.

- How do you define your priorities?
- How do you work with your team to stay focused on the critical areas and avoid distractions?
- What was the last crisis you had and how did you face it?
- How much do you delegate to save time for yourself?
- Are you clear on what is core and what is not, so that you can choose who to partner with?
- How do you work with your partners? How do you differentiate supplier from partnership relationships?

CHAPTER IX

BE THE CHANGE

The Chief Execution Officer should be the strongest change agent in the organisation. In any business, there is always the need to drive transformation to make it better. Every CEO will have to find what type and level of transformation is required to implement the vision, and to face the challenges of a market in constant change. A substantial portion of the success of any plan is to have the top leader of the organisation as the main sponsor. He must be bold, and lead the team to adjust, embrace and benefit from that environment. The CEO, in this dimension, should create the ground for change, define the key alterations needed, and be bold in its implementation. He must also understand the market context in which change is compulsory. Finally, he must create a spirit of renovation – fresh, innovative and agile as though the business is a startup.

Create the ground for change

People, in general, are reluctant to leave their comfort zone. Change is not something they would admit they like. Change generates uncertainty and risk, and it takes hard work to go through it. Therefore, the need for change should be explicit, the leader must be prepared to lead from the front and be open to being challenged. He must find out where the resistance is and who could be allies. Change agents across the organisation will be critical to the execution of those transformational plans.

You will need to fight against the corporate memory. People like to do things in the same way they've always done them. And veterans will often say that they've 'tried it before and it didn't work', which for them is justification not to try again. I found that, sometimes, it is good to forget.

Establish why change is needed

Whatever the reason for change, whether it is poor business performance or external forces out of your control, it should be made clear and visible to the people in your organisation. 70% of business change fails because the organisation has not been sufficiently engaged in the change.

Explaining the reasons for change requires a joint effort from your Engagement and Execution dimensions.

I met the newly appointed CEO of a chemical company. Their main challenge was to improve profitability in order to have a sustainable business. He had individual conversations with his top team. Some of them acknowledged the fact, but others blamed the market, suppliers or other functions. It was the same when he arranged chats with the next level down. He realised it was going to be more difficult than he had thought. There was a total lack of awareness of the level of change required. He arranged for the top two levels of the organisation, around 100 people, to come together at an event out of the office environment.

He switched off the lights. In complete darkness, he started to share the brutal facts. People started to feel uncomfortable. They did not like the lack of light. He said: "This is exactly where we are right now. We have no visibility of where we are going. We all came here today thinking 'everything will be OK', but in fact, we are lost. I need you all. It is going to be hard. If you are not ready to embark upon such a journey, leave quickly." Six months later, only half of the original team were still there. But they managed to make the transformation and get on to a path of profitable growth.

Making people understand the need for change is difficult. There are many reasons for it.

Maybe you need higher profits. The levels of return produced by your business must be attractive to the investor community. Therefore, your company should provide higher returns than other alternatives for investors. It would be a matter of survival as a company.

Or maybe the competitor landscape has become more challenging. Customers decide which companies will succeed with their buying options. If your competitors are providing better service, have more compelling offers or better propositions, you are in trouble. When disruptive players enter your market, your team need to understand that their jobs might be at risk. Thomas Friedman described it well:

> "Every morning in Africa, a gazelle wakes up. It knows it must run faster than the fastest lion, or it will be killed. Every morning a lion wakes up. It knows it must outrun the slowest gazelle, or it will starve to death. It doesn't matter whether you are a lion or a gazelle. When the sun comes up, you better start running."

It means that just understanding the necessity for change is not enough. You need to create a sense of urgency. If there is a real need for it, it must be done quickly. Small gestures can also help.

In the restructuring of a financial services company, cost reduction was an essential part of the plan. The COO stopped free coffee and bottles of water in meeting rooms. People started to complain. She said: "I know it is not an astronomical saving. However, we cannot afford to have them. This is how critical our situation is." It was an eye-opening signal for everybody that every penny counted. A small but strong signal that would encourage people to take action.

Be open to being challenged

To fully engage the organisation in change, they must see you leading it. There is no better way to show it than having open conversations in which people can challenge you and your team. Being exposed to direct questions, giving detailed explanation and your personal rationale, will help people to understand and then underpin your cause.

When we were going through a significant business transformation, I wanted to be openly challenged. So, we decided to organise a conversation with six people from different areas of the business, in which they could ask anything that was on their mind. It lasted an hour and we recorded it on video so that others could have access to the content. There were tough and direct questions. I explained the plans we were working on and why change was necessary. They wanted to know how we had got into that situation in the first place, what my personal commitment was, and the reasons why I believed in this new set of actions. It was a difficult experience as I decided to answer every question, even the most personal ones. However, it was a powerful way to show why I was behind the change.

Find the agents and the resistance points

Provoking change in a company is the role of the leadership team. However, making it happen is a task for the whole organisation. To help, you need to find those individuals who will create the same ground and environment for change within their units. There are three characteristics of great change agents:

- Credible leaders: people with a strong reputation that others will follow

- Passionate communicators: individuals capable of explaining the rationale for change intellectually and emotionally

- Resilient executors: people with determination and the ability to maintain high energy levels

I found it useful to do an exercise using quadrants to identify where your most direct team sits. It is possible to apply it to the whole organisation; you should judge to which level you want to do it.

Establish a quadrant where you have on the X-axis how engaged people are, and on the Y-axis how active they are.

CHANGE APPETITE

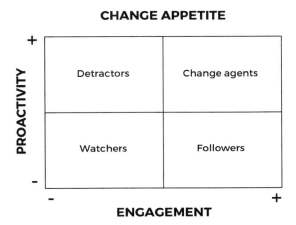

Low engagement and activity would be in the bottom left. They are the watchers – individuals who observe passively what is going on. You need them. They don't resist, they don't contribute to the transformation, but they have tasks to do.

In the bottom right you have the followers. They are not proactive, they don't lead. However, once something is decided, they will execute. Some of them, with additional motivation, will move into the change agents' quadrant.

Those are in the top right. Well engaged, ready to move and to mobilise the organisation. They are core to your change agenda. You must spend time with them, making sure they are fully aligned and getting feedback throughout the process.

The top left is the detractors' population. They don't just watch. They make negative statements about the situation, the plans and the chances for success. You will waste your time trying to convince them. I made that mistake once. Detractors are like a black hole in the universe; they will drain all your energy, with no positive results. Some of them perform important tasks in your organisation, so you might need to keep them temporarily. Others will not make the journey, so the sooner you take action on them, the better. However, make sure you listen to their criticisms at the beginning of the process. Within their negativity, there could be some proper challenges to consider when it comes to making the plans. Once the plans are decided, detractors could become a problem.

Define changes

Once the scene has been set for change, you should be specific about the changes to be made. A transformation mindset is a powerful tool for any organisation. However, it has to be focused and concentrated on the key areas to be renovated.

In any transformational plan, you will need to distinguish between big changes and small changes; you will need to review and confirm the business and operating models; you will need to reassess the skills you have in the business.

Your Execution dimension should show its best planning skills. You must make some clear decisions: discriminating what is important from what is accessory, being clear on what is the core and what is not, and what people should be great at.

This is one of the moments in which your three dimensions intersect: a clear vision, strong engagement activity and a powerful transformational plan.

Confirm the business and operating models

A big change plan can be the origin or the result of a review of your core business. It could be that a significant market shift forces you to evolve the central activity of your company. Or you could decide to move proactively to a different set of products and, hence, you will have to transform your organisation.

You must be clear with people about what your core business is. For us, in the telecoms sector, the traditional business was selling telephony services

– a line and a telephone number to make calls. It evolved to include data mobile services and, with it, myriad applications from that traditional service. Now it is all about high speeds in broadband at home or on the move. Content, films, series and sports are creating new business models. Revenues and margins are moving in the value chain. Some just disappear, others are replaced. Understanding it is not enough. Just sitting on top of legacy profits will be a risky position for those companies.

In the corporate world, change is also occurring with the move to Cloud services, pay as you go platforms and more recent associated solutions like cybersecurity. This creates the need for change in all areas of the company: products, services, cost base, people skills. It means new ways of dealing with customers, launching services faster, and leveraging the power of technology in every single activity. The operating model, internally and externally, should also be adjusted. This is making players look at themselves and rethink what their core business is and how they are organised around it.

The change in market dynamics will be affected by how your customers embrace change. It will modify the way you work with them. Your role will evolve. This generates challenges and opportunities. Your team will experiment with those and they should adjust themselves just as your company does.

A leading chemical company was supplying car paint to a large car manufacturer. The automotive company bought paint in gallons. They had many specifications to meet: the quality of the material, endurance, pantone colours, weather resistance and many more technical features. Once you were certified as a supplier, you would receive paint orders. The sales professional at the chemical company was focused on getting selected as a supplier and selling as much paint as possible. The more paint he sold, the better, and of course, delivery times were critical to avoid penalties.

One year, the car manufacturer decided to change their scope. They wanted to make the paint supplier part of their value chain. They wanted to strengthen the contribution towards the finished product, and by doing this, get more involved with the supplier and drive innovation. To do this, they defined new metrics and new ways of paying. They organised a meeting with the supplier's sales leaders and explained that they were going to pay by painted car, not by the gallon.

Suddenly, all the focus and effort of the traditional way of selling had gone. Now, the best way to generate the maximum profit for the chemical company was to use the least possible paint whilst achieving the targets defined by the car manufacturer. For sales professionals, it also changed the way they worked and dealt with the customer. In the new model, it was all about quality metrics on each painted car, how thin the layer of paint was, but also the brightness, resistance to erosion, and many other key parameters.

The challenge for you as a leader is that, regardless of the industry in which you operate, this will happen. A disruption in your operating or business model will occur. I spent a good amount of time looking at how we worked, and the new archetypes we would need. Margin shifts will give a solid guide of what to look at.

Encourage people re-skilling

One of the key changes to make is on people. Everyone will need to transform his or her attitude and skills. Many will struggle. You have a key role to play in providing them with confidence and support during this process. They should see that you also keep re-skilling yourself. The fact that you continue to learn will reassure them about their own capabilities but, more importantly, about the need to do it.

In the telecoms industry, the salesforce has been transforming considerably. People have been forced to change the way they work. This could be considered a brilliant opportunity. However, it is a difficult experience for a lot of people.

I remember a conversation with one account manager at a sales conference. He had spent over 10 years selling the audio conferencing portfolio. His main target had been to drive the maximum number of minutes possible. The more minutes, the larger the revenue and associated margin. He had to understand the dynamics of audio conferencing services. However, with the move to IP services and the growing impact of collaboration tools, he needed to manage a larger and more complex portfolio.

He told me: "Luis, this is a major challenge for me. However, I am 45 and I see it as an opportunity to reinvent myself. I am attending meetings with young newcomers who are getting some of this new stuff a lot faster. But I am determined to learn and restart. It is also exciting to see how the industry is changing, and be a part of it. But we need help, and some time to transform ourselves." He was scared, but he was ready to try. Our role was to give him the resources and time to go through the re-skilling journey.

Customer relationships continued to be important in business-to-business sales, but new skills were also required. The portfolio of solutions was broader, the sources of profit were different, and the way customers were buying was changing. We wanted to offer the re-skilling opportunity to those who were willing to take it.

With the speed of change in any industry, re-skilling becomes a critical tool for companies. Some parts of the portfolio will disappear and others will be created. Over time, companies will no longer need people to configure telephone switches but they will need security experts. Network design moves from a static defined architecture to a changing, software-defined architecture. With more automated financial processes, using robotics will free up accounting experts who, with the right re-skilling, could instead analyse data as a 'data scientist'. Organisations that can identify the new jobs of today and the future will be better prepared to succeed. They will also need to figure out the ones that will disappear, and how they plan for the transition of their workforce – who will learn new skills and capabilities, and how they will do it.

The process of launching a re-skilling programme is key in such a changing environment. When the team in our European operations decided to do it, they quickly realised it was a critical long-term activity. They called it 'Never stop learning'.

There were six key areas of focus:

- Understanding the jobs that would be required in the future

- Understanding the jobs that will no longer be needed

- Defining several training programmes for different journeys based on the profiles of new and existing skills

- Communicating it widely so that as many people as possible knew about it

- Agreeing with the individuals how to make the shift

- Executing the transition plan.

For example, an area of growing demand was security. The telecoms industry is looking for more and more security services in the network space. Security is gaining more and more facets, which need new tools and expertise, but there aren't enough people with such expertise and it is creating an inflated cost of salaries for those with that knowledge. At the same time, some of the traditional network components are being reduced, like voice networks. This creates an opportunity for those voice engineers who, with good technical capabilities, are willing to learn the security domain.

So, the team launched the programme and it was well received and used, although it took some time to get traction and speed. I learned the importance of the CEO in advocating the re-skilling of your team in a changing market.

Implement and facilitate change

Being the change agent of the organisation will demand a strong focus on implementation. You will not have the time or the skills to do it yourself, so you must facilitate an execution framework for transformation.

Making such a big transformation of a business will require a methodology to run the plans. You should define how big change is going to be industrialised and consumed. However, teams should also have the ability ilkilk—

to keep transforming their daily operations with a continuous improvement mindset. Those plans should be supported by investments in tools and training.

Your role as a facilitator in the execution should be complemented by strong engagement activity. Those two dimensions should be highly visible in this part of your journey as a leader.

Define how to industrialise and consume change

All organisations experience constant change, whether it's a series of small movements in operational models or big transformational programmes. In any case, the key to success is to create the most effective way of consuming that change. Change management is, and always will be, a key activity in any transformational project. The difference between organisations that do change well and organisations that don't is how they prepare to absorb it.

When executing any change, you should define four elements:

- Problem definition or problem statement
- Action plan
- Execution
- Tracking results

Let us discuss briefly the first two items. I found they are critical to drive execution properly. We have made references to the other two in previous chapters.

Defining the problem will save time and money

Defining the problem sounds obvious but it is very easy to skip or do it wrong. Some of the issues you observe are symptoms rather than root causes. Therefore, you could miss the actual problem. You should spend quality time on making a clear statement of the problem you aim to resolve.

In a logistics company, they were failing to deliver goods to customers by their committed dates. Customers were unhappy because they didn't get their goods on time. One way to articulate the problem could have been: 'The dates we give to our customers are too optimistic and hence we do not deliver on our promises.' Clear. There is an obvious way to address this: every sales and service rep should look at historical data before committing to a date, consult the delivery team, and agree the schedule with them. Finally, they should even add some contingency in case unexpected issues happen. All of this should, consequently, address the issue of not giving the right dates to customers.

However, have they addressed the root cause? Was that the real problem? They were providing too optimistic dates – but why? In some cases, it was because they were the standard delivery times in the industry. The sales and service teams did not want to lose business and tried to provide a competitive offer. They thought they would be able to improve internally once the business had been won. So, the actual issue was that they were too slow. The optimistic promises were just a symptom. The problem statement should have been: 'Our delivery process is too slow and to keep customers on board, we are over committing when we will deliver.'

The set of actions would then be focused on shortening the delivery cycle to provide a faster service. And there would also be some actions that involve customers – for example, providing address data with higher quality.

Solid action plans will make your life easier

Action plans take different formats depending on the profile of the organisation, and even the type of activities to be performed. However, my favourite way is to make them with a kind of 'project plan'. Project management has three basic principles: what, who and when. You can, of course, get more sophisticated on those three by asking: At what cost? What are the dependencies on another task? Which skills and resources are needed? But at the end, you will summarise what must be done, who is going to do it, and when it will be delivered by. The more precise you can be, the better outcomes you will get – and also the easier it will be to follow up.

One of our product managers was reviewing the launch of a voice over IP product with his team. It was a key base for supporting customers moving into the digitalised IP world and the product was also essential to keep us competitive in the market. When the team came up with the proposal for the project plan, most people were satisfied. But when the product manager looked at the plan, a great discussion started. One of the items of the plan was:

Task: Refine the ordering model

Owners: Will and Ahmed

Time frame: Q1

You could say that it is perfectly acceptable to have such a line in a plan to launch a product. However, he went deeper. What does 'refining the ordering model' mean? What do you want to achieve with it? If the task is so generic, knowing what you will get out of it is impossible. Each person could be expecting different end products. For some, refining could be improving the web interface; for others, it could be reducing the number of errors. It is key that in this planning process you agree as specifically as possible what the task is. Many times in my career I made the mistake of accepting a broad task description that ended in dissatisfaction and double the work. This is especially relevant when there are thin boundaries with other assignments or dependencies. It is good to have a longer, clearer descriptor like: 'Refine and simplify the ordering model to reduce by 40% the time it takes to enter data, and get to zero orders rejected in the next phase of the process when passed to production'.

Another interesting element of this task was that it had multiple owners. I always opt for having a single owner, even if others support him or her. An owner is not the person who should do everything; it is the one who carries the responsibility for making sure that the task gets done. It is also a great development opportunity. Ahmed questioned his ability to be heard in the team, and to have the power to ask others to do what was needed. Well, it is about leadership. In most large organisations you do not have all the resources you need reporting to you. Project leadership versus project management is a big differentiator in professional skills and career development.

The third piece of the task above is about timing. A quarter is a long period of time. If you are planning three years ahead, you might think it is the right measure, but for anything shorter term, it is not.

There are two ways of setting a delivery date. One is starting from where you are. Then, define the tasks needed and the dependencies. Put them together and you will end up with an estimated date. If that date is too far away, you might review the plan again in successive iterations.

The other way of planning is when you have a deadline; for example, when one of your customers needed services to begin on the same date that their contract ends with their previous supplier. In that case, you plan against that date. But it may mean that you have to make trade-offs in functionality or resources.

By having clearly industrialised plans and projects, change will happen. To make it easier to consume, you could use periodic releases. Within 90-day cycles, you could deliver a new set of modifications to processes, systems or products. They should be significant transformational items. I found it made it easier for some people to digest those elements with this approach.

Separate big changes from small changes

In my experience, change is a big play but it must be accompanied by small modifications that can accelerate improvements and provide short-term benefits. For most people, the large transformations will not be visible in their daily jobs. However, it is possible to generate some momentum and provide quick wins.

We were facing a large systems transformation that we expected to deliver good process improvements. It would take a few months before the operating units would see the positive difference. But at the same time, there were many smaller frustrations in people's day-to-day lives, which we decided to tackle in parallel. This programme was all about removing 'irritants'. These small issues had a large impact on people's daily activity. We set up a website where people could share their irritants, and we established a dedicated team to deal with them. Some irritants were discarded, but the rest were categorised into quick fixes and input for bigger system changes. Over 1,000 small modifications were made: changing old slow desktop computers, removing duplicate data entry, automating spreadsheet reporting or cleaning data to avoid billing mistakes. It was a small investment with a big return. Removing the irritants cleared the way for the larger transformation to come and made people more open to it.

Use continuous improvement to drive small change

One great tool to foster innovation and process enhancement is taking a continuous improvement approach. The 'lean' methodology is a solid way of implementing small changes. I learned how 'lean' could help customer-facing teams to work better. I have seen the impact of continuous improvement initiatives in back-office functions, producing higher quality outcomes. And I have seen how, with the right incentives and systems, it is possible to eliminate a lot of unnecessary work to check offers to customers. However, it is not necessarily relevant to the whole organisation. If you embark upon such a programme, go deeper in just a few areas and invest in great coaches.

I visited a support centre in Budapest. The teams there had been using 'lean' for over a year. The continuous improvement coaches were proud of how it had been embedded in the different teams' day-to-day work. They shared a performance dashboard and held a weekly session to review new ideas and how the previous initiatives had been implemented. I attended one of those meetings and there was a strong customer focus behind all the suggestions. Most ideas were small changes with high impact; for example, linking systems to avoid asking customers for the same information three times. The team was also following the impact of those improvements, and recognising the best performers each month. But they couldn't have worked in this way without the coaches. Over time it became a business-as-usual activity. It was a simple and powerful example of empowerment in the field.

Invest in change

You might have heard the phrase 'put your money where your mouth is'. It applies to transformation. It means you should back up your strategic direction with the right investments to support it. Information technology (IT), systems and processes are powerful and indispensable tools to drive your plans. Underinvesting is the most common mistake I have seen. The CEO should be a strong advocate of the IT role in the change agenda.

We applied those investments to different areas:

- Productivity. Smoother processes drive efficiency. More focused human intervention would save time and money. Robotics can eliminate tasks or automate them. Tools to support teamwork, collaboration and faster interactions between employees will make everybody more effective.

- Customer experience. Increased service levels with self-service functionality and innovative platforms will secure customer loyalty. The ability to capture feedback or make personalised offerings will adjust your business to your customers' demands.

- Data management. Better information management will give you stronger control of your company, whether in financials parameters, customer understanding or market understanding. Knowledge will allow you to make faster, better decisions and react quicker to the unexpected.

You should work out where your biggest bets are in terms of investments to drive change. Whatever you decide, focused money will accelerate the transformation.

I had regular reviews with our IT team to make sure we kept our investment plans on track. Having support and focus from the CEO made a big difference to them and their plans.

Understand the market

Market dynamics are one of the fundamental reasons for change, so you should keep an eye on what is happening in your company's market environment. Your customers' decisions might be changing as they face new challenges. The company you lead should adjust to those dynamics. They offer new opportunities and create threats.

Your competitors will be moving. The traditional ones will get better but new ones will come. Some will disrupt how you make money today. Knowing them well will be an important task for you. Scanning the ecosystem around your business will be exciting and rewarding at the same time.

The CEO of a bank organised weekly hour-long sessions to review specific areas of technology and how they could impact them. He invited leading technology companies and startups. He listened to their business models and how they dealt with customers. He had meetings with venture capital firms to understand where they were investing. Round tables with employees helped him to capture new ideas. He was obsessed with learning as much as possible about what was happening in the market. His team prepared simple explanations of deeply technological issues for him and his team. In an iterative process, those conversations were used to refine his current plans, open new projects, define pilots and create collaboration initiatives with startups. The CEO was the change engine, leading by example in creating market awareness.

Build the company for the market opportunity

By understanding your customers in depth, you will be able to create an organisation ready to work with them as well as for them. In a corporate environment, when you talk to your customers' CEOs, they will give you guidance. You have the opportunity to listen and learn about their CEO dilemmas on a variety of topics.

I discussed with many of them about how they managed their operations. They function in a global environment but everyone is headquartered somewhere. They might also have customers who live and work in a specific location. In that sense, those are local operations. This is where you must create the balance between being global and acting locally, or vice versa. I decided to call it 'Glocaland', a new territory. I shared it in a speech at a business school, addressing newly graduated students. I invited the audience – MBA students in marketing, sales and communications – on a journey to this recently discovered territory: Glocaland, the land where global and local meet.

I spoke about concepts like:

- Glocal markets, created by the global expansion of multinationals which need a strong local touch to serve their customers. Customers become glocal because they expect global account management and services from their suppliers, and at the same time, the ability to deliver and contact them locally.

- Glocal sourcing, which allows companies to manufacture or provide services across several locations which are more convenient for them, 'making the world flat' (*The World is Flat* by Thomas Friedman).

- Glocal talent is the key differentiator between good companies and great ones. How to find, attract, retain and develop the best talent available (both for global and local roles in the organisation) is the real challenge. Only those who are able to do it will succeed. Organisations need glocal managers who will have people in several countries but who will enable them to execute as a single team.

We adjusted our organisation to be glocal: global governance and support of processes, products and customers, balanced with local presence and customisation according to regulation or specific needs. Collaboration and strong leadership are key to a successful implementation. I constantly experienced this dilemma of being global or local. We tried to bring to life the well-known expression 'thinking globally and acting locally'. It is a difficult balance which requires bold decisions and a flexible team.

Prepare for a world of prosumers

One way to understand the market is to interact directly with the end users of your services. Technology is diluting the traditionally clear borders between the professional world and the personal environment. A new generation of consumers are using innovative tools to gather product knowledge and make more informed decisions. They are ready to share more personal interests and opinions, and they trade private data for services. At the same time, a fresh wave of 'digital natives' professionals with long-standing inherited consumer habits are joining our companies. The CEO should know and be open to the so-called prosumers': professional consumers.

Prosumers are challenging obsolete ways of working. As a result, we need new ways of thinking in order to assure security and the protection of critical assets.

Prosumers are thought-provoking for any leader. Whether they are customers or employees, they foster stimulating debates. However, they will demand solutions as well. Attracting them as clients or talent will mean changing processes, mindsets and tools. I found it refreshing to talk to them and look at which areas we were ready to adjust. You must also be clear that others will not change.

Identify the successful disruptors

That people-based disruption caused by prosumers is also happening with companies. New players are creating innovative solutions with different business models that could make your company tremble. And existing companies are even entering into different markets with a big impact on other sectors.

As with the CEO of the bank I referred to previously, your role is to understand the dynamics. Talk to as many people as you can. Learn who is doing what, and why. How they plan to make money, how they will capture their customers, and what is their unique selling point. Understand and discuss how your customers will react.

Then, you will be ready to act. Of course, this is not a one-time job. You should be doing this as part of your daily activities.

A leading software player was launching an evolution of their solutions. They aimed to add functionality in collaboration tools to their basic electronic mail services, and they were considering telecommunication companies as partners in their rollout strategy. However, one of the new features of their platform was to offer free phone calls to their customers. Unintentionally, they were entering as a disruptive competitor against their main partners. It made them reconsider their plans about which services to deploy.

You can find disrupting players in almost any industry. This is an unstoppable process. Taxi organisations, hotel consortia, banks and content producers are all experiencing how the market is being disrupted. In many cases, regulation is overtaken by the speed of imagination. As a CEO, you should never hide behind it. Good, innovative ideas will find their way.

There are different ways to look at disruption and how it works. Companies like BMW create an ecosystem of innovation around them. IBM is always searching for new ideas and frequently acquires that incremental knowledge. Barclays foster Fintech discussions to understand and invest in what could be their next generation of services.

It is important to systematically scan what is going on, because not everything goes well. You don't need to react to every disruptive idea that plans to make a breakthrough in your business.

I spend a few hours a week reading and talking to people about disruption. Learning from the telecoms industry was interesting. New solutions based on software-defined networks challenged existing products and forced the whole industry to think about how to embed them. However, I found it just as enjoyable to learn about disruption in other industries. And you, as the custodian of your company's vision and its future, should reserve time to disrupt your own business.

Become a digital leader

Our world, and the way we live and do business, is embracing digital technologies faster than ever. We are attached to mobile devices and, increasingly, to wearables which help us to take care of our health. The content that we absorb is progressively through digital channels. Booking trips or restaurants, completing banking transactions, buying goods and services are more digital than ever. The abundance of connected devices in our homes, businesses and cities generates a huge amount of data, which creates opportunities. We could go on and on. The best CEOs will be those who can understand and leverage the value of digitalisation. They should become digital leaders.

Under your Execution dimension, you should master how digital technologies are being used. You must be surrounded by people with deep knowledge of how they work, and what you can do with them. Partners should keep you informed and updated when it comes to what they see as best practice. Looking at where investors are placing their bets in new companies is good practice. Also look at the startups hosted in incubators, and why they are there.

As a digital leader, the CEO should challenge the team on how they use technology. The Chief Information Officer role should evolve to become the Chief Digital Officer. Moreover, marketing leaders must understand how to leverage big data techniques and digital channels. Operational managers should look at ways to improve efficiency by using sensors and robotics. The CEO should encourage this activity, making sure that proper funding is available to them.

We used to have discussions on what was next in our industry. In our portfolio roadmap reviews, we discussed other competitors and new players, and how we were preparing to compete. However, we also left space to pilot innovative services. Testing use cases for holography, or using voice-activated devices to develop a digital assistant, triggered the excitement of the team. By doing this, you get a view of the art of the possible. It doesn't need to become a product or service. Awareness alone was very important to me. The CEO will be better if combined with a digital leader. Some are good role models, like Ana Botin. I have met her several times and I enjoyed her perspective about what it means being digital.

Ana Botin is the Executive Chairwoman of Santander, the leading financial group of the Eurozone. She decided to face the industry's challenges and transform the organisation to make it more competitive, serving customers who are, like the rest of the world, changing fast. She and her team are leveraging the power of digital technologies and driving a cultural change with the customer at the centre. Innovating in products and services, investing in digital platforms, attracting new talent and re-skilling their people are all core elements of the strategy. Their plans address the challenges of improving efficiency, responding to new players trying to disrupt the role of banks, and balancing risk, regulation and growth.

Santander has a special character with a strong customer focus, social contribution, and commitment to economic development where it operates. Ana is a visible digital leader and is the chief advocate of the transformation of a bank, created in 1857, which has learned to evolve, to maintain its global leadership position. She is always vocal, clear and inspiring in internal and public speeches.

Act as a startup

You are the only one who can drive a startup mindset throughout your organisation. Your entrepreneurial skills should flourish to create a new way of thinking and acting, developing an environment in which ideas can flow, decision making is agile, and implementation is focused on results. Bureaucracy is removed systematically, failure is permitted as a source of learning, and talent can innovate. You can influence and make it possible by setting the organisation's culture and behaviour from the top. In today's world, combining a strong heritage with a fresh attitude can deliver excellent results. If you are already the CEO of a startup, make sure you keep that feeling from the first days of your business.

Heritage is all about the customer base, sector expertise and brand reputation, which can build confidence and sustainability. However, new generations have a higher risk appetite and are ready to try products, services and companies if they are convenient. Balancing both profiles is an important part of the strategy.

The CEO should make sure that the business keeps reinventing itself. Decision making could become a competitive advantage, enabling you to execute at pace. Your startup mentality should result in unlimited curiosity and desire to explore what is possible.

Keep reinventing your business

Startups lack corporate memory. On one hand, this is good as it allows you to face challenges with an open mind and, probably, out-of-the-box thinking. However, it also means that the founders can lack experience. You should aim to achieve the same out-of-the-box thinking, combined with your existing company knowledge. Use what you know but don't let it become a blocker.

The CEO of an Italian car insurance company shared his views in one of our meetings. Insurance is a well-established industry with clear parameters on how actuarial calculations are made. They have improved their cross-selling capabilities and started using big data techniques to assess their customers better. However, the availability of information about how customers drive, thanks to car sensors, is changing the entire sector. New offerings such as 'pay as you go' policies are appearing. Depending on how much or how fast you drive, you would be charged differently. They recognised the challenge this would bring to their business model. All previous models would no longer be valid. So they decided to acquire a company specialised in car sensors, to learn more and develop new services for their customers. They had to reinvent themselves without losing their core business.

Either you recreate yourself, or someone else will. The CEO plays a critical role in driving this approach. These new initiatives' ways of working will be different from your existing business. You need to find the best way to push for reinvention, depending on your organisation. How and when you reinvent your business is something you must think about carefully, or it could be too late.

We held a market-leading position in a specific solution for financial services customers. However, we realised that the integration of new Cloud services could be an opportunity but it could also disrupt our business. So, we decided to acquire a startup specialised in that area to complement our portfolio and be prepared for our customers.

Make decision making a competitive advantage

Making decisions quickly is one of the biggest challenges in big corporations. In my conversations with CEOs, they always talk about their attempts to drive more agility. Be bold. Making quick choices, and being prepared to reverse them if they were wrong, is a new capability required in a fast-moving market. You might have suffered the corporate disease of endless debates until the group reaches consensus. Of course, you can always find more facts, and more people to get involved, whether it's a decision related to a customer offer, a new product feature, or a new investment. But speed is of the essence. Making quick decisions does not mean they are less robust.

The CEO must be the first one to keep this mindset. We had a meeting about a supplier negotiation; there was a long discussion about end features, and requests to the shortlisted contenders. The challenge to the team was to reduce the decision-making process from three months to three weeks. When we looked at the reasons why it was taking three months, we found we could shorten everything. It was done. The suppliers were happier, even those who lost, as we saved them time. We made savings sooner and we learned how to be more effective in those processes.

Have unlimited curiosity

Exploring what happens around you is one of the best ways to learn. It is also a powerful attitude when it comes to understanding what others do. The best tool for exploration is questioning. You should develop a good ability to ask questions. Interrogating in a consistent way will make you more knowledgeable. As we said before, to develop this habit, you just need to be curious. Most startup founders I have met like to ask as much as they tell.

Every single conversation is an opportunity to learn. You should instil this behaviour across your organisation, making it easier for people to present answers to questions, allowing them to build projects outside of their day jobs, and creating a systematic way of thinking out of the box.

We wanted to encourage innovation and improve customer service. Clearly, the day jobs were not covering everything. So we created a competition called The Challenge Cup. It was launched with the ambition to address problems or opportunities faced by people across the business. Projects were focused on a specific customer issue. They got a higher score if they had members from different parts of the business, to promote collaboration. Several hundreds of teams competed every year. Many of them worked like startups. Even they had to get the funding to execute their propositions. There was an official winner each year. However, there were rewards for all those projects that reached completion. Most ventures started out with the curiosity of a few individuals, and their appetite to deliver a better service to customers. It was an inspiring way of aligning thousands of employees' energy. I learned the power of the desire to go the extra mile for your customer. You just need to find the best way to channel it for the better.

Reflection

The Chief Execution Officer must be a change agent. In this dimension, your boldness and entrepreneurial skills should be some of the core capabilities to develop.

- Are you a change leader? How do you explain the change needed in your organisation?
- How do you separate big changes from small ones?
- Do you facilitate change in the way you work? How?
- How do you develop your market understanding of customers and competitors?
- What are you doing to be a digital leader?
- Is agility a key objective for you? Why?
- What startup attributes do you like? Do you think you could embrace those in your business? How?

CONCLUSION

I wrote this book with the intention that the three dimensions we discussed would be useful to you. You might be a seasoned CEO of a large multinational, or a recently appointed CEO of a smaller company or a startup. You might be next in line, or have the ambition to be a CEO in the future. You might be leading a team or a unit as a 'mini-CEO', or just be curious and interested in what it means to be a CEO. It doesn't matter; those three dimensions apply to you.

We discussed the core skills associated with each one. We presented a few key areas where you would need to use several of those capabilities, and some areas where one dimension is more visible than others. And we have seen, as well, how those dimensions interrelate and reinforce each other. To excel as a CEO, you should aim to master the core skills supporting those dimensions. Your determination will be the basis to succeed.

Personally, I found the Evangelist dimension the hardest one to develop. It made me really consider my core values and capabilities. This set of skills is more related to who you are. By reflecting on them I learned a lot about myself. Once you work on them, they become the cornerstone of how you will perform.

The Engagement dimension is the one I enjoyed most. I draw my energy from being with people from different profiles, leading a team or spending time with customers. Those conversations are also unique learning opportunities.

The Execution dimension made me feel proud. This is where the outcome of your role will be visible. The sense of achievement you feel and the heritage you build are at the core of why you wanted to be a CEO.

I hope that while you were reading, something has clicked in your mind. Maybe a new idea, a reassurance, even the determination to change something.

I enjoyed being a CEO, leading a team and working with customers. I can promise you, it is a tough but fascinating journey on which you never stop learning.

Even when reading its final version, I continued to discover areas I could do better, and elements of the dimensions I enjoyed. More and more stories came to my mind. But also new ways of working I want to try and develop.

I would like to keep the conversation going around what it takes to be a great CEO, an amazing leader. So, I would love to invite you to share your stories and discuss your ideas and themes at: **the3dceo.com**

Thank you for taking the time to get this far, and enjoy the journey.

NAVIGATION GUIDE

CHAPTER I.
DISCOVER THE THREE-DIMENSIONAL CEO

Understand the three-dimensional CEO

Know why you want to be a CEO

CHAPTER II.
DEVELOP THE CORE SKILLS OF THE 3D CEO

II.I. EVANGELIST DIMENSION. YOUR INNER SKILLS

II.I.a STRATEGIC THINKER

II.I.b OBSESSED

II.I.c POSITIVE

II.I.d PASSIONATE

II.I.e BALANCED

II.II ENGAGEMENT DIMENSION. YOUR CONNECTION SKILLS

II.II.a INSPIRING

II.II.b CURIOUS LISTENER

II.II.c HUMBLE TO LEARN

II.II.d EMPATHETIC

II.II.e CONNECTED

II.III EXECUTION DIMENSION. YOUR EXECUTION SKILLS

II.III.a FOCUSED

II.III.b BOLD

II.III.c UNREASONABLE

II.III.d ENTREPRENEUR

II.III.e RESILIENT

CHAPTER III.CREATE A VISION

Define what you want to achieve

Articulate the vision

Bring together your organisation around an image

Drive consistency

Mobilise cathedral builders

How we applied the story

Connect with dispersed teams

Make the vision real

Support your people managers

Co-create the vision with the market

Challenge the vision externally

CHAPTER IV. ENGAGE

Communicate relentlessly

Define the message

Use storytelling

Choose the communication channels

Make events memorable

Identify and remove communication blockers

Deal with cultural diversity

Listen as much as you talk

Use the four most powerful words for engagement: What do you think?

Listen through mentoring

Be visible; get out of the ivory tower

Master the art of people recognition

Remember to say thank you

Recognise the invisible people

Communicate with all stakeholders

Engage through the power of being positive

CHAPTER V.
LEVERAGE THE POWER OF THE TEAM

Select the team

Identify your 'extended' team

Develop the team

Benefit from the value of a diverse team

Acquire talent

Develop talent

Organise the team

Coach the team

Be ready to have tough conversations

Empower the team

Make clear that empowerment comes with accountability

Apply consequence management

CHAPTER VI.
BUILD CUSTOMER OBSESSION

Make customers visible internally

Lead by example

Put yourself all in

Learn to say no

Develop the art of working with customers

Collaborate to serve global customers

Listen to customers; it is the best sales tool you have

Create business opportunities

Pay attention to small things that really count

Learn from customers

Ask "what can we do better?"

Put service at the heart of your team

Learn why you win and why you lose

Prepare to win

Know why you lose

Inspire and be inspired by customers

Understand customer innovation challenges

CHAPTER VII.
DRIVE HIGH PERFORMANCE

Define clear expectations

    Explain how you work

    Set clear targets

    Pay attention to detail

Track performance

    Hold inspiring business reviews

    Create a can-do attitude

    Use paradoxical thinking to resolve conflicts

Master information management

    Establish key business indicators

    Identify how you look at data

    Classify your data: Quadrants

    Simplify by managing by lists

    Use waterfalls to describe the hydraulics of the business

Evaluate individual performance

    Create formal and informal feedback moments

    Be bold on improvements

    Replicate success

Connect the dots

    Encourage sharing

    Stimulate cross-fertilisation

    Use curiosity to drive collaboration

CHAPTER VIII.
STAY FOCUSED ON EXECUTING THE VISION

Prioritise

  Plan your first days

  Separate what is urgent from what is important

  Learn to say no

Simplify

  Remove unnecessary work

  Build trust

  Make a simpler organisation

Keep calm

  Assess the impact

  Address root causes

  Develop a learning culture, not a blaming one

Delegate

  Bring decisions close to the customer

  Create mini-CEOs

  Master risk management

Learn to partner

  Establish your core

  Build partnerships, not supplier relationships

  Leverage the ecosystem

CHAPTER IX.
BE THE CHANGE

Create the ground for change

  Establish why change is needed

  Be open to being challenged

  Find the agents and the resistance points

Define changes

  Confirm the business and operating models

Encourage people re-skilling

Implement and facilitate change

Define how to industrialise and consume change

Defining the problem will save time and money

Solid action plans will make your life easier

Separate big changes from small changes

Use continuous improvement to drive small change

Invest in change

Understand the market

Build the company for the market opportunity

Prepare for a world of prosumers

Identify the successful disruptors

Become a digital leader

Act as a Startup

Keep reinventing your business

Make decision making a competitive advantage

Have unlimited curiosity

ABOUT THE AUTHOR

Luis Alvarez Satorre has spent over 30 years in leadership roles. Ex-CEO of BT Global Services, a global telecommunications leader, he has previously worked for Ericsson, IBM and Santander Group. Working in a changing sector driven by the forces of digital technologies has allowed him to connect with business leaders from many companies around the world. He has led significant improvements in business performance, transformation in customer experience, the development of innovative solutions, and he has built winning teams. His passion for the business and the lessons learned inspired him to write this book.

Luis is an active contributor to social media, where he shares his thought leadership. He regularly attends the World Economic Forum, speaks at conferences and runs a radio programme called CEO Conversations for Radio Capital in Spain.

As a digital advisor, Luis is supporting companies with their growth and development agendas, where digital technologies are transforming their businesses. He is also acting as strategic advisor to several leading startups in areas like cybersecurity and Fintech platforms, and to private equity firms.

A passionate engineer, Luis graduated with a Masters' in Telecommunications Engineering from Universidad Politécnica, Madrid. He completed his business education in Tuck University, IMD and ESADE.

Married to a brilliant telecom engineer, they have four children, all of whom also have Masters' degrees in Engineering. They enjoy exploring about how technology can be used to make the world a better place.